Pagan Portals

Osiris

Raising the Djed Pillar

Olivia Church PhD

London, UK
Washington, DC, USA

First published by Moon Books, 2026
Moon Books is an imprint of Collective Ink Ltd.,
Unit 11, Shepperton House, 89 Shepperton Road, London, N1 3DF
office@collectiveinkbooks.com
www.collectiveinkbooks.com
www.moon-books.net

For distributor details and how to order please visit the 'Ordering' section on our website.

ISBN: 978 1 80341 518 5
978 1 80341 519 2 (ebook)
Library of Congress Control Number: 2025931368

A CIP catalogue record for this book is available from the British Library.

Design: Lapiz Digital Services

UK: Printed and bound by CPI Group (UK) Ltd, Croydon, CR0 4YY
US: Printed and bound by Thomson-Shore, 7300 West Joy Road, Dexter, MI 48130

What People Are Saying About

Osiris

Osiris, more authentically called Wesir, is one of the most important Ancient Egyptian gods. He is king of the afterlife but also has power over agriculture and the fertile black soil along the banks of the Nile. In *Pagan Portals - Osiris*, Egyptologist and practicing pagan, Dr Olivia Church, combines meticulous scholarly research with insights from a modern spiritual perspective. This is a superb book and a must-read for anyone wanting to learn more about the Egyptian pantheon and ways to honour this ancient deity whose mythology includes life, death and rebirth.
Lucya Starza, author of Pagan Portals titles *Candle Magic, Poppets and Magical Dolls, Scrying,* and *Rounding the Wheel of the Year,* as well as the Gothic novel *Erosion*

Olivia Church has produced a much-needed volume about the Egyptian deity, Osiris. While we find the market packed with books about Goddesses, there is relatively little about male deities. Once again, as in her previous books, Isis (2021) and Sekhmet (2022), Church gifts us a book that is well balanced with her scholarly background alongside her views as a modern Polytheist. She generously provides references and the book has a structure that flows with the information until you have the full picture. This is more than an introductory book; it is a proper foundation to meet Wesir, or Osiris as Greeks translated his name, the Egyptian Great God of Agriculture and Afterlife. This book is a must on your bookshelf if you are studying the Gods of Egypt, whether you are a Pagan, or not. 5 stars.
Ness Bosch, author of *Sacred Bones Magic Bones*

Contents

Also by Olivia Church

Pagan Portals – Isis
Great of Magic, She of 10,000 Names

Transcending cultures and time to meet ancient Egypt's universal Goddess of magic, life, and death

978-1-78904-298-6 (Paperback)
978-1-78904-299-3 (e-book)

Pagan Portals – Sekhmet
Lady of Flame, Eye of Ra

An invitation to come face to face with the incarnate female power of ancient Egypt

978-1-78904-713-4 (Paperback)
978-1-78904-714-1 (e-book)

Norman Lanz (31.10.1949 – 26.01.1991)
and
Jasper Hugh Hall (30.10.1956 – 08.02.1994)
May your names always be remembered.

Abbreviations

CT – Coffin Texts
PT – Pyramid Texts
BRP – Bremner-Rhind Papyrus
BD – Book of the Dead (i.e. the Book of Coming Forth by Day)

Timeline

(Dates provided by Shaw, 2003)

Early Dynasty Period

Comprising Dynasties 1 & 2, 3000-2686 BCE

Old Kingdom

Comprising Dynasties 3–8, 2686-2160 BCE

First Intermediate Period

Comprising Dynasties 9 & 10, 2160-2055 BCE

Middle Kingdom

Comprising Dynasties 11–14, 2055-1650 BCE

Second Intermediate Period

Comprising Dynasties 15–17, 1650-1550 BCE

New Kingdom – (Including Ramesside Period)

Comprising Dynasties 18–20, 1550-1069 BCE

Third Intermediate Period

Comprising Dynasties 21–25, 1069-664 BCE

Late Period

Comprising Dynasties 26–30 & 2nd Persian Period, 664-332 BCE

Graeco-Roman Period

Comprising Macedonian & Ptolemaic Dynasties, 332-30 BCE
Roman Period, 30 BCE – 395 CE

Map of Featured Ancient Egyptian Sites

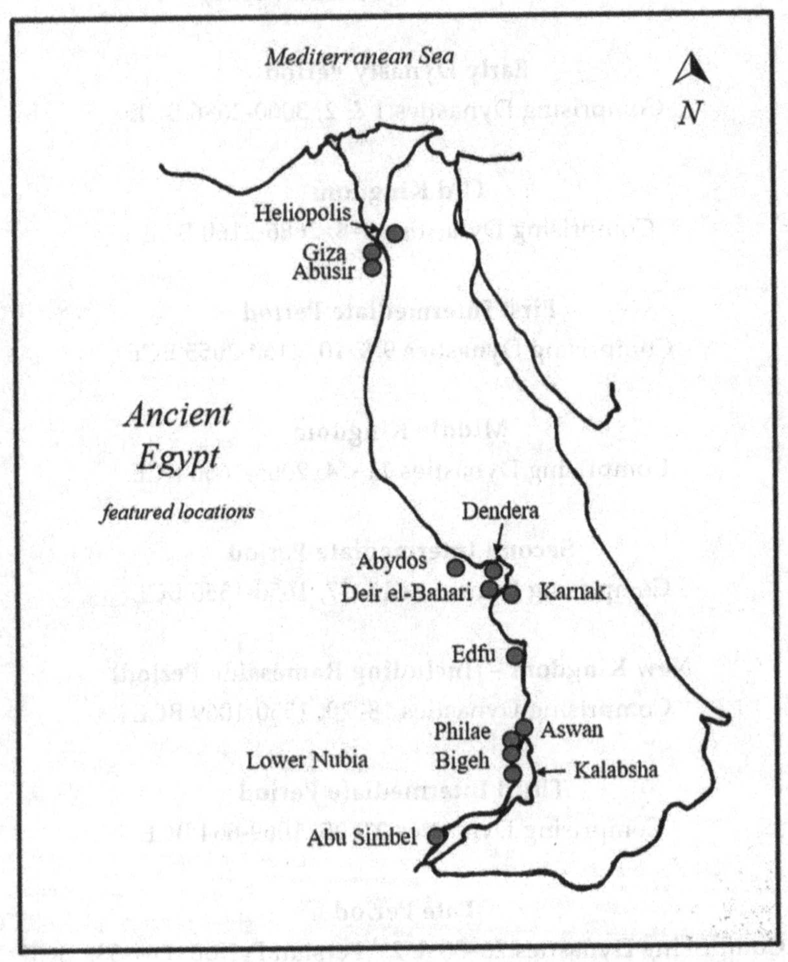

Preface

This book will introduce you to Osiris, known to the Egyptians as *Wesir,* God of agriculture, the soil of the Black Land, King and Great Judge of the afterlife. This is a deity who is close to my heart, slumbering beneath the earth we tread and residing firm within the bones of our bodies. He is there whether we are cognizant of him or not. This book is an offering to Him and an opportunity for readers (and myself) to learn more about this mysterious and ancient deity. Within these pages I offer knowledge informed through my degrees in Egyptology, as well as insights gained through my own contemporary Pagan worldview. I have endeavoured to keep the distinctions between these two realms of knowledge clear throughout, with citations to historical knowledge provided and personal gnosis and modern Pagan interpretations stated as such.

I always recommend to anyone who finds themselves drawn to the ancient pasts of Egypt and Nubia to also learn about the cultures and people who reside in these landscapes today. There is so much knowledge and beauty to be found in listening to the experiences of modern Egyptians and Sudanese people living along the same Nile as their ancestors. Let us ensure that our love and interest in the *Netjeru* (the Gods) of these lands is reflected in the interest, respect, and care, that we extend to the descendants who reside there today. I offer up my humble thanks to these people whose ancient and modern cultures have profoundly touched my life.

Additional thanks should be given to my friends Donna, Chris, Pam, and Dee for their unfailing support and kind words which have lifted me from the realms of self-doubt and motivated me to push forwards. I also wish to thank my second cousin, Caroline, and my mother Heidi, for their extensive research into our family history, allowing me to know more of my ancestors.

Though he passed before I could meet him, I have often thought of Norman and his beloved Jasper during the writing of this book. It took longer than I expected to finish this project – with several life milestones crossed before I reached the end – so I thank my editor, Trevor, for his patience and faith in me. As ever, I also want to thank my husband and best friend Thomas for his constant encouragement and love, and for bringing me copious cups of tea – and our cat Moaki, for his healing purrs.

Before we start, I need to explain the ancient Egyptian words that I will use throughout this book. Firstly, unless quoting translations, I will call Osiris by his Egyptian name which is commonly rendered *Wesir* (*wsjr*). This is probably pronounced something like, 'oo-seer' (although the translation and pronunciation of 'Wesir' remains contested and inconclusive amongst scholars). Increasingly these days I recommend using the Egyptian names of the *Netjeru*, not only because spoken and written words contain *heka* (*ḥkꜣ*), loosely defined as 'magic'; but also, because it makes a lot more sense to use the names that the Egyptians knew their deities by, rather than those translated into a foreign tongue. The Greek translations of these names are better known today as early Egyptologists could read ancient Greek before they ancient Egyptian. Fortunately, however, this is no longer the case. That said, this book's title uses the Greek name, Osiris, as it remains more recognisable to a wider audience. It is hoped that those drawn to this deity find this book, and upon reading its contents, become more familiar with the Egyptian names for the Gods and Goddesses. For convenience, I will also use the term 'Osirian', when referring to certain concepts or traditions, as there is not an equivalent term in Egyptian (of which I am aware, at least).

I will also often use the Egyptian word *Netjer* (*nṯr*) for a single male deity and *Netjeret* (*nṯr.t*) for a single female deity (pronounced 'neh-cher' and 'neh-cher-et', respectively). For plural female deities, *Netjerut* (*nṯr.wt*, pronounced 'neh-cher-oot') may be used; for plural male deities or a group of mixed gender deities the word appears as *Netjeru* (*nṯr.w*, pronounced 'neh-cher-oo'). These are capitalised as proper nouns and are transcribed into anglicised spellings for ease of reading. Don't worry if this feels a bit complicated – you won't have to memorise this as the intended meaning will be obvious in the context of the text itself.

Please also be advised that, as Wesir is a deity who is intrinsically associated with the afterlife and mortuary cults, this book will make repeated references to the subject of death, though it does not intend to explore this in great detail beyond Wesir's ancient context and continued relevance.

Introduction

Known to the Greeks as Osiris, the Egyptian deity Wesir has his roots deep in the origins of ancient Egyptian civilisation. He was (and is!) a complex deity with a rich history stretching up from Sudan, Nubia, and Egypt, and spreading out across the Mediterranean taking on culturally specific forms as his cults travelled. To the ancient Egyptians, Wesir was the king and judge of the afterlife, the embodiment of all deceased pharaohs and, eventually, all deceased people who had passed through the perilous paths of the *Duat* (the afterlife realm). As the pre-requisite to afterlife was re-birth, Wesir also represented rejuvenation, with his own life, death, and rebirth reflecting the cycles of nature, as clearly observable in Egypt's landscape. As shown by his famous mythology, Wesir was deeply connected with the Nile's waters, soil, and riverine life. Like his beloved sister-consort Aset (Greek Isis), Wesir was also a deity whose mythology related to significant human experiences which applied to all Egyptian people, rich or poor, king or farmer. Many experiences appearing in his mythology, though presented in a fantastical form, remain pertinent for people in the modern day.

Wesir's post-mortem iconography is instantly recognisable even to those with minimal familiarity with Egypt's ancient Netjeru. He is depicted with a long, curved beard, wearing the *atef* crown – the tall white crown of Upper (southern) Egypt, flanked by the addition of two ostrich plumes – signifying his sovereignty over life and death, of both Egypt and the realm of the dead (O'Connor, 2011, p. 41). He holds the Crook and Flail indicating his role as the watchful shepherd of his people, as well as one with the means to exact judgement and punishment, if necessary. Most often Wesir is clothed in white mummiform wrappings and painted with green, blue, or black skin, reminding us of both his Nilotic death and his association with the fertile powers of nature (fig. 1). Sometimes Wesir can be also depicted with the head of a ram, representing his syncretised form with the Sun God, Ra, when the pair merged in the underworld realm (van Dijk, 1986, p. 9). Like many other Egyptian Gods, Wesir is described as having a 'body of white gold' and a 'head of lapis lazuli', precious materials to his ancient worshippers and ones that furthered his association with the Sun God (van Dijk, 1986, p. 9).

Relief depicting Wesir in the Tomb of Sennedjem, Dier el-Medina
Photograph by Olivia Church, 2017

The Black Land

As with any other ancient Egyptian deity, Wesir's nature, mythology, and worship is firmly rooted in Egypt's north African, Nilotic landscape (though he can, of course, be worshipped anywhere). It is perhaps safe to say that the majority of his modern devotees (though not all) reside outside of Egypt, and yet the call of the Nile continues to draw them towards this land. Through the name 'Osiris', Wesir's worship travelled beyond Egypt, following the cults of his divine consort, Aset. More commonly in the Mediterranean, however, Wesir became part of a composite deity known as Serapis (see Chapter 4). Despite the Mediterranean context of the Isiac cults of Isis and Serapis, the landscape of Egypt remained of the utmost importance to their devotees abroad, as is evident in the iconography, literature, and material culture they left behind. Though re-interpreted through a Graeco-Roman lens, the European devotees of Wesir and Aset never forgot their north-African origins.

Today Egypt is known to Egyptians as Misr مصر (or, more officially, the Arab Republic of Egypt). To their ancestors, the land was referred to as *Kemet* (*km.t*), the 'Black Land', amongst other names. This referred to the black, fertile soil that made up the banks of the Nile River (Brewer and Teeter, 2007, p. 22). Naming their land after this rich band of soil emphasised its importance to the Egyptians of the past, as it continues to be to this day, providing food and foliated shade in a valley surrounded by desert sand and rocky mountains. The Nile has been a source of life for Egypt's earliest inhabitants far into prehistory and has continued to draw in people and cultures from all directions, seeking its life-giving resources, forming a complex multi-cultural history. The Nile River is fed by two tributaries known as the 'White Nile', originating in Lake Victoria (surrounded by Uganda, Kenya, and Tanzania), and the 'Blue Nile' from Lake Tana in Ethiopia. Flowing from south to north, the rivers meet in Sudan and from there travel up through Upper Egypt, Middle, and Lower Egypt in the North, spilling into the Mediterranean Sea from Egypt's Delta. According to Wesir's mythology (see Chapter 1), the Nile's currents continued to flow through the sea, carrying him to Byblos in Lebanon.

The Nile and its black soil taught the Egyptians about the cycles of life and death through its annual flooding and recession. Each year, around July or August by the Gregorian calendar (or sometimes between June and September), melting snow from Ethiopia would flush down the Blue Nile, causing the banks of the united Nile to flood. This would wash the land with red silt, causing considerable damage to river-side settlements. This silt, however, also revitalised the land and, as the waters receded, it left behind fertile soil in which to plant crops in the cooler months of the year (Brewer and Teeter, 2007, pp. 21, 31). The area of the floodplain was believed to be the realm of Order, ruled by Wesir and his heir, Heru (Greek Horus) and this was the land where the Egyptians built their homes and their Pharaohs governed in accordance with *ma'at* (truth and order). The realm beyond this, occupied by desert, mountains, and non-Egyptians, was the realm of Chaos ruled by Wesir's brother, Sutekh (or Set, known to the Greeks as Typhon). Here, dangerous animals, daemons, unknown forces, and unknown peoples dwelt. The Nile's cyclical flooding continued annually for millennia until the building of the Aswan High Dam in the late 20th century. Though this Dam regulated the waters and minimised repeated damage to settlements and historic monuments, it should not be forgotten that it also displaced thousands of Nubian people, who are still affected by this today.

Egypt in the 21st century is a land which clearly juxtaposes the ancient with the modern, and everything in-between. Modern Egyptian life continues to be intimately tied to its Nilotic landscape. People continue to work the fertile fields, yielding its gifts; they traverse the Nile on riverine boats, fishing and travelling upon its waters; traditional crafts and foods are created each day; folk customs carry echoes of Egypt's multicultural history; the Muslim call to prayer rings out several times a day, echoing the ritual patterns of the past; and Coptic masses keep ancient words alive. Egyptians today are increasingly celebrating and reclaiming their noble past from those who would disinherit them, and many continue to live in close relationship with the land. Describing her bodily connection with her Egyptian homeland, feminist author Nawal el-Saadawi wrote:

> *'I was proud of my dark skin. It was a beautiful brown, the colour of silt brought down to my land by the waters of the Nile.'*
>
> (el-Saadawi, 2018, p. 7).

As well as tying her the natural rhythm of her home, this description is also deeply reminiscent of surviving depictions of Wesir, whose skin colour likewise represented the hues of the Nile Valley's fecund water and earth.

Origins

Though we cannot be certain that the cult of Wesir existed in the Predynastic and Early Dynastic periods due to an absence of, or very limited traces of writing, there is a tantalising possibility of early cults. Images of rulers (or at least clearly elite leaders) from this time are shown wearing the curved beard and the white crown (the *Hedjet*) and holding emblems which were later held and worn by Wesir; furthermore, burials at this time certainly suggest a belief in royal afterlife, which became the primary jurisdiction of Wesir (Adams and Ciałowicz, 1997, pp. 17–18, 33). Nevertheless, conclusive evidence of Wesir's origins remains out of reach. What we *do* know is that when Wesir appears in the 5th Dynasty, the texts infer an already well-developed mythology; here, he is intrinsically linked with the funerary sphere and remains so for the duration of ancient Egypt's polytheistic history (Smith, 2017, p. 8).

The earliest written attestation appears in non-royal contexts in elite tombs from Saqqara and Giza (although obtaining a secure date for these is challenging; Smith, 2017, pp. 117–123, 161). Wesir's first written appearance in royal sources comes from a fragment from the 5th Dynasty pyramid temple of Djedkare Izezi in Saqqara (Smith, 2017, p. 114). Here, the name is written with the throne and eye hieroglyphs. Other places show orthographic variation, reversing the signs or later adding the phonetic mouth-sign to indicate the 'r' sound (fig. 2).

Common orthography for Wesir's name in hieroglyphs

Wesir's name appears more substantially in the *Pyramid Texts* of the 5th Dynasty, and it is interesting to note that his name appears without the usual determinative for a deity, with some speculating that this implies a particular emphasis on his regal role, as King of the Dead (David, 2018, p. 261). The *Pyramid Texts* are found inscribed on the walls of several Old Kingdom royal tombs in Saqqara (such as Unas, Teti, Pepi I, Merenre, Pepi II, and Queen Neith; Allen, 2015, p. 1). These texts functioned as ritual liturgies and spells to ensure the deceased successful arrival in the afterlife, which was, at that time, a privilege reserved only for kings and queens (with few possible exceptions). Though they date to the 5th and 6th Dynasties, their mythic and religious content is so well-developed that it is likely that the beliefs they convey originated much earlier (Malek, 2003, p. 102).

The remainder of this introductory book will stretch across time to delve into the character and worship of Wesir in ancient times and the modern day. Chapter 1 will explore Wesir's ancient mythology and why he is known as a Netjer of life, death, and rebirth. Chapter 2 will address his vital role in funerary religion, establishing how his mythology became manifest in ritual, and how it remains relevant to modern devotees today. Chapter 3 is dedicated to examining the curious afterlife books, which provide maps through the *Duat* and reveal secrets ordinarily left unseen. Chapter 4 provides information about sacred sites dedicated to Wesir and his cults, both within and outside of Egypt. This leads on to Chapter 5 which draws attention to ancient and modern festivals and rituals involving Wesir. Chapter 6 provides examples of ancient and modern spells and prayers which can be used in Wesir's veneration today. The book will end with conclusions summarising key aspects of Wesir's character, mythology, and worship in antiquity and the modern day. All sections begin with historical information and conclude with contemporary Pagan perspectives, illustrating Wesir's enduring relevance and continued existence in the world, within and far beyond Egypt's Nile Valley.

Chapter 1

Mythology

Wesir's mythology can be divided into two primary sections: the Heliopolitan narrative of his birth and earthly rule, and his demise and resurrection. The latter also holds details about his continued existence as sovereign of the Afterlife and his perpetual existence thereafter.

The Heliopolitan Creation Myth

Heliopolis, known in ancient times as *Iunu,* was a city located northwest of modern Cairo and was the cult centre of a group of nine deities which we refer to today as the Heliopolitan Ennead (Egyptian 'Pesdjet', '*psḏt*'), of whom Wesir was a member. The Ennead comprised Atum (one of many Netjeru credited with Creation), his offspring Shu and Tefnut, their offspring Geb and Nut, and their offspring, Wesir, Sutekh, Aset, and Nebet-hut (Greek Osiris, Typhon, Isis, and Nephthys). This sometimes included a tenth figure, Heru, as the third born son of Geb and Nut (Heru-Wer, Horus the Elder), or as the son of Wesir and Aset (Heru-sa-aset, Horus son of Aset or the Greek Harpocrates).

According to *Pyramid Text* utterances 527 and 600, Atum parthenogenically created Shu and Tefnut (who personified air and moisture), who in turn united to create Geb and Nut. Geb embodied the earth and Nut the sky; however, *Coffin Text* 76 tells us that the pair were quite literally inseparable – the sky completely covered the body of the earth with no space in between to allow life to thrive. As the embodiment of air, Shu stepped between the couple, lifting Nut's body away from the earth and into the heavens above (Pinch, 2002, p. 175). This is beautifully captured in ancient Egyptian artwork with Nut's starry body arched over a reclining Geb (sometimes with evidence of his passion reaching up towards her), separated by Shu lifting Nut aloft. Once separated, life could begin to grow between the heavens and earth, and thus emerged the offspring that the pair had conceived.

The Greek historian, Plutarch, elaborates upon the Egyptian narrative, as he so often does, alleging that the creator God, Ra cursed Nut, forbidding her from giving birth on any day of the year, until Djehuty won five extra days through winning a board game with the moon deity (Ra is named Helios, Nut, Rhea, and Djehuty – commonly known as Thoth – he names Hermes). With these five additional days of the year (now totalling 365), Nut was able to give birth to her divine offspring (Plutarch, *Isis and Osiris*, 12). And so it was that Wesir came into being, first born son of Geb and heir to his earthly kingdom:

'The foremost of his brothers,
The eldest of the Nine Gods,
Who set Ma'at throughout the Two Shores,
Placed the son on his father's seat.
Lauded by his father Geb,
Beloved of his mother Nut...'

(*The Stela of Amenmose*, 9)

Marriage to Aset

Though there is a plethora of Egyptian sources detailing the mythology of Wesir, it is important to note that the most popular linear narrative of his marriage, death, and rebirth, comes from Greek authors. Ancient Egyptian mythological sources seldom provide complete narratives all in one place, requiring us to piece together a plot that forms a coherent tale. The Greek historians Diodorus Siculus and Plutarch provide us with the best known, albeit Hellenised, version of Wesir and Aset's coherent mythology. Following the tradition of their divine elders, each of Nut's offspring were divided into pairs, with Wesir coupling with Aset, and Sutekh with Nebet-hut. Wesir and Aset's union is first attested in the 6th Dynasty *Pyramid Texts,* dating back to the very early days of recorded Egyptian history. Plutarch's narrative adds the detail that the pair's love began in the womb, regarding theirs as a union of deep affection:

> *'Isis and Osiris were enamoured of each other and consorted together in the darkness of the womb before their birth.'*
>
> (Plutarch, *Isis and Osiris,* 12)

The *Stela of Amenmose* describes how Wesir inherited the throne of Geb and his earthly kingdom, and how he maintained the balance of life and *ma'at*:

> *'Geb's heir (in) the kingship of the Two Lands,*
> *Seeing his worth he gave (it) to him,*
> *To lead the lands to good fortune.*
> *He placed this land into his hand,*
> *Its water, its wind,*
> *Its plants, all its cattle.*
> *All that flies, all that alights,*
> *Its reptiles and its desert game,*
> *Were given to the son of Nut,*
> *And the Two Lands are content with it.*
> *Appearing on his father's throne,*
> *Like Re when he rises in lightland,*
> *He places light above the darkness,*
> *He lights the shade with his plumes.*
> *He floods the Two Lands like Aten at dawn,*
> *His crown pierces the sky, mingles with the stars.*
> *He is the leader of all the gods,*
> *Effective in the word of command,*
> *The great Ennead praises him,*

> *The smaller Ennead loves him.'*
>
> (*The Stela of Amenmose*, Louvre C286; trans. by Miriam Lichtheim, 1976, p. 83)

This beautiful excerpt from the *Great Hymn to Wesir* portrays Wesir not only as an effective, well-loved ruler, but also as a life-giving deity who maintained the balance of nature.

With Aset at his side as queen, the pair cared for all living things and taught humanity how to sow seeds and grow crops along the Nile floodplain:

> *'... Isis had discovered the fruit of both wheat and barley which grew wild over the land along with the other plants but was still unknown to man, and Osiris had also devised the cultivation of these fruits...'*
>
> (Diodorus Siculus, *Library of History*, 1.14)

Theirs was a happy reign in accordance with *ma'at*. Diodorus also writes that Wesir was 'laughter-loving' and 'of a beneficent turn of mind'; instead of seeking war and battle, he led campaigns intent upon, 'visiting all the inhabited earth and teaching the race of men how to cultivate the vine and sow wheat and barley' (Diodorus Siculus, *Library of History*, 1.17). Thus, Wesir sought to spread knowledge of agriculture and a peaceful way of life.

Returning to Wesir's story, Plutarch shares an elaboration of the myth revealing an affair between Wesir and Nebet-hut. In this version,

> *'Osiris in his love had consorted with her sister* [Nebet-hut] *through ignorance, in the belief that she was Isis... the proof of this* [was] *in the garland of melilote which he had left with Nephthys...'*
>
> (Plutarch, *Isis and Osiris*, 14)

According to Plutarch, Nebet-hut exposed the infant outside in fear of Sutekh's wrath; her sister Aset, however, discovered and saved the baby. This jackal-headed child of Wesir and Nebet-hut became Aset's 'guardian and attendant', and was thus named Inpu (Greek Anubis), pledged to 'protect the gods just as dogs protect men' (Plutarch, *Isis and Osiris*, 14). This part of the narrative only appears in much later versions of the myth and it is uncertain where it came from, whether Plutarch learned of it through Egyptian informants, through Graeco-Roman initiates of Isis, or through his own invention.

The Death of a God

Following this period of idyllic rule, comes the events of Wesir's death, which, though critical to his mythology, are omitted in the Egyptian sources. This avoidance was noted by Diodorus Siculus, though the details had since been revealed by the time he heard of them:

> *'Although the priests of Osiris had from the earliest times received the account of his death as a matter not to be divulged, in the course of years it came about that through some of their number this hidden knowledge was published to the many.'*
>
> (Diodorus Siculus, *Library of History*, 1.21)

According to the version dictated by Diodorus Siculus, Wesir's brother Sutekh was the cause of his early death. To the Egyptians, Sutekh ruled over the unknown lands of the desert, wielding the power of storms, and overseeing the creation of metal weaponry crafted from the contents of his desert mines. Sutekh is a fascinating deity who was respected by the early Egyptians; however, from the *Pyramid Texts*, he emerges guilty of fratricide (Pinch, 2002, p. 192), which was repeatedly emphasised by later Graeco-Roman portrayals. Though he possessed many riches himself, having sovereignty over mined metals and previous gems, Sutekh nevertheless coveted the realm of Wesir. According to Diodorus Siculus:

> *'When Osiris was ruling over Egypt as its lawful king, he was murdered by his brother Typhon* [Sutekh], *a violent and impious man; Typhon then divided the body of the slain man into twenty-six pieces and gave one portion to each of the band of murderers, since he wanted all of them to share in the pollution and felt that in this way he would have in them steadfast supporters and defenders of his rule.'*
>
> (Diodorus Siculus, *Library of History*, 1.21)

Plutarch elaborates on the murder further:

> *'Typhon, having secretly measured Osiris's body cand having made ready a beautiful chest of corresponding size artistically ornamented, caused it to be brought into the room where the festivity was in progress… Typhon jestingly promised to present it to the man who should find the chest to be exactly his length when he lay down in it… Osiris got into it and lay down, and those who were in the plot ran to it and slammed down the lid, which they fastened by nails from the outside and also by using molten lead. Then they carried the chest to the river and sent it on its way to the sea through the Tanitic Mouth* [a branch of the Delta].'
>
> (Plutarch, *Isis and Osiris*, 13).

He explains that Wesir's body was rent into pieces when Sutekh discovered his coffin washed ashore (Plutarch, *Isis and Osiris*, 8). When Aset hears of this tragedy she 'at once cut off one of her tresses and put on a garment of mourning' (Plutarch, *Isis and Osiris*, 14).

It is at this point that the Egyptian sources pick up the narrative again. The most complete Egyptian version of the myth of Wesir comes from the aforementioned *Great Hymn to Wesir*, recorded on the *Stela of Amenmose*, dating to the New Kingdom and now residing in the Louvre. The hymn skips past the fatal deeds of Sutekh and goes on to describe how Aset went in search of the body of Wesir. The deliberate omission of Wesir's murder is owing to the ancient Egyptian belief that to record something in text or image was to give it form and permanence. As Wesir's rebirth was considered essential, Egyptian texts skip the description of his death to ensure that it is not made permanent through the power of writing. The circumstances of his death would be culturally known and were not required to be put in writing; however, the recording of his rebirth in textual form gave it permanence and manifestation.

In agreement with the Egyptian sources, Plutarch continues his narrative by describing how Aset set off in search of the body of Wesir. His version has Aset discover the chest of Wesir encased in a wooden pillar within a palace in Byblos (an ancient city located in modern Lebanon). Following a tale of magic and confrontation here, Aset returned the pillar containing Wesir's body to Egypt and wept when she saw her beloved inside. Hereupon, Diodorus Siculus and Plutarch agree that Sutekh discovered the return of Wesir's body, and tore it into fourteen, sixteen or twenty-six pieces, requiring Aset to scour Egypt in search of them (Plutarch, *Isis and Osiris*, 14–18; Diodorus Siculus, *Library of History*, 1.22). In the form of a kite (appropriately a carrion bird) Aset:

> *'... sought him without wearying,*
> *Who roamed the land lamenting,*
> *Not resting until she found him...'*
>
> (*Stela of Amenmose*, Louvre C286;
> trans. by Miriam Lichtheim, 1976, p. 83)

In all accounts Aset is successful in locating each piece of Wesir's body (see Chapter 4); however, according to the Greek authors above, 'Of the parts of Osiris's body the only one which Isis did not find was the male member' (Plutarch, *Isis and Osiris*, 18; concurred by Diodorus Siculus, *Library of History*, 1.21-22).

Rebirth and Afterlife

As a great healer and magician, Aset possessed the ability to temporarily revive Wesir into full life, before enabling his passing into eternal afterlife. Aset 'gathers up his flesh' (Hart, 2005, p. 117) and replaces his missing member with a consecrated replica (Plutarch, *Isis and Osiris*, 18). Together with her sister Nebet-Hut and the embalming God, Inpu, they conduct funerary rites to restore Wesir to life long enough for he and Aset to conceive an heir. The Greek sources appear to shy away from the notion of post-mortem conception, with Plutarch inferring that their son was already around at this point (Plutarch, *Isis and Osiris*, 18). However, this is pivotal to the Egyptian version, as it proved that Wesir was truly resurrected in all capacities:

> '[Aset] *made a shade with her plumage,*
> *Create breath with her wings.*
> *Who jubilated, joined her brother,*
> *Raised the weary one's inertness,*
> *Received the seed, bore the heir,*
> *Raised the child in solitude,*
> *His abode unknown.'*
>
> (*Stela of Amenmose*, Louvre C286;
> trans. by Miriam Lichtheim, 1976, p. 83)

This is also a recurring visual motif in religious art with scenes depicting Aset in kite form, hovering above Wesir's erect member (fig. 3).

The Conception of Horus, Temple of Dendera
Photograph by Olivia Church, 2017

Wesir's ability to create life from death is essential to the ancient Egyptian worldview. From the quiet darkness below Egypt's black soil, following a seasonal period of agricultural death, life remerged in springtime. From the swallowing of the sun at sunset and the absence of the sun's light at nighttime, the sky mother Nut rebirthed the sun at dawn. The God of agriculture demonstrated that not only is life reborn into the afterlife realm of the *Duat*, but it is also re-manifested in the land of the living. Wesir conceived his heir prior to his departure, ensuring that his line would continue to rule Egypt, rather than yield to the chaos of Sutekh's usurpation.

Aset, Nephthys, and Inpu carried out the first mummification and 'Opening of the Mouth' rituals upon Wesir, reconstituting his physical body, preserving it for eternity, re-animating it, and awakening his *ba* (interpreted as a spiritual body), ready for its journey to the afterlife. Upon his successful arrival, Wesir became ruler of the *Field of Reeds*, ready to receive the dead and judge them worthy of joining him in everlasting life, or not (see Chapter 3).

The myths go on to detail the trials and tribulations of this heir, Heru-sa-aset (Horus son of Isis), as he contends with Sutekh for the throne. Eventually Heru succeeds and rules over Egypt, with all living rulers becoming the embodiment of Heru on earth, who then become Wesir upon their demise. The tale recounted above is the most widely known and, arguably, most important myth relating to Wesir, whose elements are pieced together from the *Pyramid Texts* of the 24th-23rd centuries BCE to the Greek retellings of the 1st century CE.

A Contemporary Pagan Perspective

A contemporary understanding of Wesir's mythology is shared in my *Pagan Portals* book on Aset/Isis. Here, I explained my interpretation that Wesir is a God intimately connected with the cycles of nature and the agricultural cycle of planting, growing, and harvesting, and of birth, life, death, and rebirth. 'Just as the fields are harvested and die, so must Osiris be born anew', with Sutekh 'scattering his parts like seeds across Egypt' (Church, 2020, p. 27). It is poignant that various versions of Wesir's mythology involve his drowning in the life-giving waters of the Nile and that later additions mention that his phallus was lost to the river, perhaps ensuring its continued fecundity through the interment of his fertilising member. To me, Wesir's cyclic death and rebirth reflect the natural world and though obviously tethered to Egypt's Nilotic landscape, the cycle of life, death, and rebirth is observable across the planet.

Many contemporary Pagans maintain a close relationship to the cycles of the seasons within their homeland, with this passage of time marked by festivals and celebrations that mirror the vicissitudes of human life. Spring and summer festivals often celebrate creative energy and love; autumn and winter observances may be more introspective and a time for remembering the ancestors and the beloved dead. The cycle of Wesir's mythology can be easily translated onto the cyclical landscapes of his devotees across the world today. For Pagans with a pantheistic inclination, Wesir is a deity who can be seen recumbent in the black earth, emerging with the green shoots of springtime (see Chapter 2), growing tall to be severed as the golden grains of harvest, and floating within an arm's reach just beneath the current of flowing rivers.

Not only is Wesir's cycle relevant to people across geographies in an agricultural or seasonal sense; it is also, of course, relevant in relation to beliefs in continued or renewed life after death. For some, observing this annual death and re-growth in nature may confirm their own beliefs that the same thing happens to one's soul and/or consciousness. For peoples worldwide, throughout documented history, such a belief has been a deeply embedded comfort, testifying to the enduring relevance of funerary deities, such as Wesir. To me, it is significant that Wesir ultimately remains in the Afterlife realm, as shown by his perpetually mummiform iconography. On the one hand, his presence there ensures the permanence of the space, that the afterlife is continuously blessed by his (after) life-giving powers and will always be available for the dead to pass into. On the other, it conveys an awareness that, though life is cyclical and our loved ones can return for periods of time (according to ancient Egyptian cosmology), the dead remain in the other world and cannot fully return to us exactly as they once were. Though a sobering thought, this known reality brings an understanding to the ancient Egyptian concept of death which many of us can appreciate today. We can come to terms with the fact that the beloved dead cannot return as we once knew them, but that we may perhaps still be able to sustain a relationship with them, nonetheless, as they are never truly gone.

Beyond this life-death-rebirth cycle, though ever-related, other aspects of Wesir's mythology illustrate the elite Egyptian concern of royal succession. This is perhaps less vital to most people today, though it was of central importance to Egyptian state religion. To the Egyptians, royal succession ensured the maintenance of the cosmos, as the king was believed to be the physical embodiment of Heru (and other state deities) on earth. And so, as the Osirian cult grew in influence, the sovereign would be legitimised through their identification with Heru, and their deceased father with Wesir. The pharaoh's mother, embodying Aset, was the divine throne upon which the sovereign sat. As modern Pagans don't typically expect a sovereign to maintain the balance of the cosmos on their behalf, this concept may be less literal to devotees today. However, the concept of familial inheritance and caring for the wellbeing of the next generation might remain pertinent. Aset and Wesir's love and endurance seek to safeguard their family and though hardships are experienced, they ultimately prevail.

Chapter 2

God of Life & Vegetation

Perhaps one of the most widespread misconceptions about the ancient Egyptians is that they were obsessed with death. This is understandable, given the fact that a huge amount of surviving evidence from ancient Egypt are elite tombs, their artefacts, and funerary texts. Though Egyptian settlements and domestic remains have also survived, they are vastly outnumbered and overpowered by the dominance of – and our modern fascination with – funerary structures and treasures. Even many temples are often accompanied by mortuary temples or have a necropolis nearby. Whilst this has a lot to do with a preservation bias (stone structures and deliberately interred items survive better than mud-brick settlements and their discarded domestic detritus), you have to also ask *why* such effort was exerted towards securing an eternal afterlife? Perhaps the ancient Egyptians went to great lengths to ensure that they reached the Afterlife because they never wanted life to end? Maybe it was not death with which they were enamoured, but *life*. Of course, the two are inescapably intertwined. Understandably, then, Egypt's principal deity of death, Wesir, has also been repeatedly referred to as God of life and vegetation as well.

Readers will doubtless come across many references to Wesir as a nature and fertility deity, with various scholars suggesting that he was an early vegetation deity from at least the Predynastic or early Dynastic periods, pre-dating the written record (though without textual sources, this is hard to prove; Smith, 2017, pp. 107–114). Despite this, more recent scholarship has moved away from describing Wesir in this way and increasingly emphasise that grain and vegetation functioned as metaphors for Wesir's funerary rebirth and resurrection, rather than the other way around (Betrò, 2024, p. 16). Wesir is centrally a deity of death and rebirth; however, Wesir's association with natural fecundity cannot be ignored, and it plays an important role in his revived veneration in the modern day. Even if perceived through a predominantly funerary paradigm, Wesir is undoubtedly associated with the restorative waters of the Nile and its resulting agriculture.

The Nile Flood

In most cultures, but especially those located amidst vast expanses of desert, water is greatly valued and celebrated for its life-giving power. From Egypt's earliest religious texts, Wesir was associated with this source of life. The ancient Egyptians gave the River Nile various names depending on the attribute being described. Its destructive capabilities during the inundation were personified by the Distant Goddess (Sekhmet or Tefnut), whereas the fertilising result of the flood was personified by the God, Hapy. Representing fecundity, Hapy was depicted with river-blue skin and a full, curvaceous body, oftentimes carrying the Nile's agricultural yield or pouring sacred water from offering *hez* vases. In some sources, Hapy's waters were credited as aiding Wesir's resurrection (Pinch, 2002, pp. 136–137). Elsewhere, Wesir appears to consecrate the water through the presence of his own immersed body.

As described in the previous chapter, Plutarch recounted the myth of Wesir and his watery demise in the Nile, drowning in a coffin following the machinations of his brother Sutekh. Though not articulated as vividly in Egyptian texts, the association between Wesir's body and the Nile appear to have a long provenance within Egyptian religion. Though Wesir is alleged to have died within its waters, his contact with it produced the belief that the Nile had the power to restore life. The Old Kingdom *Pyramid Texts* equate the Nile's annual inundation with the arrival of Wesir, who comes to rejuvenate Egypt's crops:

> *'Osiris is come, the flood with provisioning arm...'*
>
> (*PT Pepi II*, utt. 690; Allen, 2015, p. 288)

In addition to this, the floodwaters also appear to restore life to the deceased king, who is ritually purified by Nile water which flows from Wesir's body, conferring the immortality of Wesir upon them (Delia, 1992, p. 183):

> *'You have your water, you have your inundation, the outflow that comes from the god, the decay that comes from Osiris. Your arms are washed and your ears are cleaned out: this controlling power is "akhified" for his ba.'*
>
> (*PT Pepi*, utt. 436; Allen, 2015, p. 109)

The *Pyramid Texts* also describe Wesir as the *Wadj-Wer* (*wꜣḏ-wr*), the 'Great Green', which was a name for the sea (*PT Teti* 366), appropriate considering the typical green of Wesir's skin in artwork.

Prior to his mythic death in the river, Wesir was lauded as the one who, alongside Aset, taught humanity the skills of agriculture. According to early Egyptian mythology, Wesir and Aset taught the early Egyptians how observe the seasonal timings of the annual flood to determine when to plant and harvest its abundant yield. In 1977, William Darby, Paul Ghalioungui, and Louis Grivetti appropriately titled their co-authored volume about ancient Egyptian cuisine, *Food: The Gift of Osiris*. When one considers the invaluable gift that grown food is to our survival, and how vastly the agricultural revolution changed the course of human history, it is impossible to regard Wesir as a God of death only, for food is the stuff of life.

Grain and Barley

In addition to being associated with the water of the Nile, Wesir was also identified with the fertile soil along its banks, with texts naming him as 'him of the mud' (*PT Neith*, utt. 665A; Allen, 2015, p. 319). The colour of Wesir's skin appears to be is intentionally related to this, appearing either as black, like the fertile soil, or green, like the crops that sprout from it. The earliest written text directly associating Wesir with agricultural yields appears in the *Ramesseum Dramatic Papyrus* of the 12th Dynasty (*c.* 1950 BCE), where he is likened to the harvested barley, beaten by animals on the threshing floor (Geisen, 2012, p. 72). This is curious considering the myth of his dismemberment by Sutekh, who often takes the form of an ass – an animal used in such agricultural activities.

References to this connection to crops recur throughout ancient Egyptian history. In the *Coffin Texts*, he is equated with the grain God, Nepri, where he states, 'I grow as the living Nepri' (*CT* 330; Ragueh, 2016, p. 1). In a funerary text from the 26th Dynasty, Wesir is credited as the creator of barley, which 'sprouted from Osiris' limbs when Thoth placed it in the embalming hall' (Wagner 2016, p. 350, III, col. 65–67 and pp. 337–45; III, col. 18–39). This is artistically represented in an image painted on the inside of the 21st Dynasty coffin of Nespawershefi, where Wesir is shown lying on a funerary bed with the rays of the sun shining down upon him, causing plants to germinate from his body. The image makes it clear that this takes place whilst he is located within the realm of the *Duat* by the decoration of stars upon the bed in the shape of the hieroglyph for *pt* 'sky', and the presence of two conjoined sphinxes representing the entry and exit to the *Duat* (the western and eastern horizons) above him (Roberts, 2000, p. 37, pl. 28). From the afterlife, Wesir is therefore shown growing plant life from his body.

Ancient mummiform figures filled with corn seeds, known as corn mummies, have been found in various sites across Egypt and are a manifestation of the idea of life growing from death (Centrone, 2004). These are figures, shaped in the mummiform image of Wesir, and formed from sand, earth, or clay, and grains such as barley, were often laid within a miniature coffin. These appear to have been used in the cult of Wesir where, according to inscriptions at the temple of Dendera, the mummies would be created, watered to germination, and buried as a part of the Mysteries of Wesir during the season of *Peret* (the planting season), in the month of *Khoiakh*. These mummies are found in various sites, deposited in temple complexes by priests, and possibly in other sacred sites by individual devotees (Betrò, 2024, pp. 2, 15). Whilst corn mummies appear to have had a cultic role, 'Osiris beds' appear amongst New Kingdom funerary equipment. These consisted of wooden boxes with a figure in the form of Wesir inside, filled with Nile silt and barley seeds (Shaw and Nicholson, 2008, p. 239).

An intriguing parallel to the practice of corn mummies is known from ancient Greece, where during the ritual mourning of Adonis at the *Adonia* festival, Athenian women would carry wooden images of Adonis up to their rooftops and plant quick-growing seeds in 'Adonis Gardens', before letting them wither in the sunlight (Håland, 2023, p. 432). Though culturally distinct, the concept of planting quickly germinating seeds in containers representing a deceased God (or in Adonis' case, an apotheosised figure) is interesting to consider.

The planting of quick-growing seeds in shallow vessels towards the end of the New Year continues to be a ritual practised by Coptic Christians, perhaps as a memory of ancient rituals of renewal and 'Osiris beds' (Darby, et al, 1977, p. 167); the New Year for Coptic Christians occurs in autumn, in association with the ancient agricultural calendar's month of *Khoiakh*.

God of the Vine

As a deity with a purview over agriculture, in addition to grain and barley, Wesir was also associated with viticulture, which is depicted in Egyptian art since the Old Kingdom (though its production predates this). In the *Pyramid Texts* he is named, 'the Lord wine-coloured with supplies' (*PT Pepi I*, utt. 442; Allen, 2016, p. 112) and 'Lord of Wine [who] is in flood' (*PT Pepi I*, utt. 577; Allen, 2015, p. 186). Some scholars have surmised that a sympathetic connection was observed between red wine and the colour of both Wesir's blood and the Nile's floodwaters (Poo, 2009, p. 153). A papyrus residing in the British Museum shows a grapevine hovering before an enthroned Wesir (BM EA10471,21), with its position floating in front of the God's nose indicating the vine's life-giving, restorative power (Guasch-Jané, M. R., et al, 2013, 158). Grapes are a recurring motif in New Kingdom tomb art seeking to encourage such regenerative power for the deceased interred therein (Poo, 1995, pp. 150–151). In addition to this, wine – typically red wine – was a common offering made during temple and funerary offering rituals, with scenes showing the 'Offering [of] wine to the Lord of Eternity, so that he may act like Ra Every day' (*Tomb of Horemheb*; Poo, 2009, p. 61).

Wesir's association with wine continued into the Graeco-Roman period, with Diodorus Siculus recording that:

> *'... the discovery of the vine, they say, was made by him near Nysa, and that, having further devised the proper treatment of its fruit, he was the first to drink wine and taught mankind at large the culture of the vine and the use of wine, as well as the way to harvest the grape and to store wine.'*
>
> (Diodorus Siculus, *Library of History*, 1.15:8)

Nysa was the mythic birthplace of Dionysus, whom the Greeks equated with Wesir (see Chapter 4).

God of Nature and the Earth

As the son and heir of the earth God, Geb, some sources describe Wesir as the body of the earth itself. For example, inscribed upon a piece of ostraca, now housed in the Cairo Museum, is a hymn to Wesir where he appears as the bearer of the earth, supporting the sky, who causes the earth to tremble when he quivers (evocative of both his Heliopolitan father and grandfather, Geb and Shu). Further, the hymn evokes Wesir as the spine of Egypt, carrying Egypt (and the world) upon his back:

'If canals are built...
If one builds estates and temples,
Moves monuments, makes fields,
Excavates tombs and graves,
They lie on you,
You are the one who does this.
They are on your back,
More than can be written about.
There is no empty space on your back.'

(Roberts, 2000, p. 34)

Thus, this hymn designates everything built upon the land as resting on the spine of Wesir. Alternatively, one might read this more metaphorically, that Wesir shoulders the weight of Egypt, as its ruler; his back, symbolised by the Djed Pillar, represents stability and strength and this hymn may indicate that, rather than embodying the earth, Wesir is the stability of Egypt.

Through conceived through a 1st century BCE Greek perspective, Diodorus Siculus claimed that the 'men of Egypt' regarded Wesir and Aset (Osiris and Isis) as 'the sun and the moon', explaining that the name 'Osiris' meant 'many-eyed', 'for in shedding his rays in every direction he surveys with many eyes, as it were, all land and sea'. He goes on to credit them with governing the cycles of nature:

'These two gods, they hold, regulate the entire universe, giving both nourishment and increase to all things by means of a system of three seasons which complete the full cycle through an unobservable movement, these being spring and summer and winter; and these seasons, though in nature most opposed to one another, complete the cycle of the year in the fullest harmony.'

(Diodorus Siculus, *Library of History*, 1.11)

A Green Afterlife

The Egyptian concept for the desired afterlife paradise, the *Sekhet-Iaru* (*sḫt-j͗rw*), 'Field of Reeds', was a fecund place that represented an idealised Egyptian landscape. It was a perfected reflection of the earthly realm, located within the broader underworld realm of the *Duat* (see Chapter 3), and it is depicted as ever-green and foliate, with rivers and growing crops kept fecund through Wesir's ever-rejuvenating presence there. As this afterlife was thought to mirror that of life on Earth, the deceased would carry on as before, though with the status of the Blessed Dead (the *akhu*). As such, scenes of the Field of Reeds show, the deceased – or, preferably, their servants – resuming work by sowing and ploughing the fertile fields, continuing to raise food provisions for the Gods (Taylor, 2001, pp. 34–35). Just as the soil along the Nile had to be tended, so too did its afterlife equivalent, overseen by the divine shepherd and agriculturalist King, Wesir.

As expressed elsewhere, Wesir continued to be fertile in death, fertilising the cultivation with his life-giving water, raising plant-life from his body, and demonstrating his continued virility within the earth through ithyphallic iconography. Though considered primarily a funerary God, to the Egyptians, this role was clearly tied to earthly fecundity and perpetual renewal. So, a God of death he certainly was, but undoubtedly, a God of life also.

A Contemporary Pagan Perspective

Amongst my most treasured memories of visiting Egypt for the first time in 2017 is the memory of travelling along the Nile by means of felucca. I vividly remember gazing into the water, glistening from the sun above, staring into its deep blue face and contemplating Wesir's existence below the waves. This deeply sacred, ancient river has provided the people and creatures along its banks with the means to live in a land surrounded by striking desert. Its annual flooding wrought destruction and plague, as well as life and prosperity. Today, its flooding has ceased since the creation of the Aswan Dam, displacing Nubian people from their ancient homeland, and the water is no longer safe to drink without high levels of sanitisation (like most urban rivers today). Nevertheless, the Nile retains its striking beauty and fertile gifts, sustaining life in the eleven countries it flows through, with Egypt being its exit into the Mediterranean Sea. To me, Wesir's essence continues to drift by in its currents. To travel along the river, speaking prayers to Wesir, and carefully decanting its water for its magico-religious use is to partake in an ancient ritual that has retained its spiritual potency into the modern day.

Many modern Pagans will be familiar with the concept of living and dying Gods, of nature deities who emerge from the sprouting foliage, thriving with earthy virility, and who eventually succumb to the mysteries of death, retreating into the dark earth to await rebirth. Much of contemporary Pagan mythology is inspired from works such as James George Frazer's *The Golden Bough*, within which the similarities between the living and dying Gods Adonis, Attis, and Osiris (Wesir) are considered. Here, Frazer speculated that such myths related to observable natural phenomena (Frazer, 1993, pp. 424–425; Vickery, 1973, p. 56). Though Frazer's work may not be considered historically robust, this observation is nevertheless applicable to the mythic cycle of Wesir. For those seeking divinity in the natural world, this interpretation may continue to make sense and transcend cultural and temporal boundaries. Outside of Egypt, many of us can observe tiny green shoots sprouting from black soil in our farms, gardens, or house plants; we can share in the excitement of their growth, before witnessing their inevitable withering and retreat. We then eagerly we await their return the following year, all the while remembering the cycle of Wesir. He reminds us that even though the soil is cold and dark, and life appears absent and silent, there is activity below the ground. Wesir lies waiting, his body prepared, gathering seeds, before reaching skyward when the spring returns. Despite the vast distance in geography and time, Wesir's mythic cycle can easily be projected onto the cycles of the seasons, should modern devotees wish to explore that (see Chapter 5).

Though many Egyptologists today may strongly affirm that Wesir was a predominately funerary deity, his fecund, earthly, lively associations with growth and agriculture are undeniable. There is, of course, a major emphasis on Wesir as the ruler of the afterlife, but all stages of the cycle of life, death, and rebirth, are equally imperative. As the bringer of agriculture and its cyclic renewal, Wesir brings humanity the precious resource that is food and, to me, this makes him a vital God of Life, as well as death.

Chapter 3

God of Death & Rebirth

As stated in the previous chapter, the Egyptians greatly valued and celebrated life and sought to ensure that it continued into perpetuity. For this reason, beliefs and rituals surrounding death were important throughout the duration of Egypt's ancient culture. Regarding early evidence of afterlife beliefs, in *Following Osiris*, Egyptologist Mark Smith cautions against jumping to conclusions that assume that burying human remains or including grave goods in burials necessarily indicates a belief in an afterlife (Smith, 2017, pp. 9–10). What *does* suggest such beliefs, however, is attempts to deliberately *preserve* remains, for what other purpose could this resource-demanding and time-consuming task serve? The oldest evidence we have for this comes from the Predynastic cemetery of Hierakonpolis, in Upper Egypt (Smith, 2017, p. 40). Textual evidence confirming beliefs in the afterlife then arise in the Old Kingdom *Pyramid Texts*. Belief in continued consciousness after death, therefore, stretches across Egyptian prehistory into the modern day. There is much to say about ancient Egyptian beliefs and traditions relating to death and the afterlife and so this chapter will focus on the most central concepts and those relating to Wesir.

Wesir is intimately connected to the funerary sphere from as early as the *Pyramid Texts*. These texts make recurring references to the 'Imperishable Stars', referring to a belief that the deceased monarch would ascend to the heavens, like Wesir, to become an eternal star within the body of the sky Goddess, Nut:

> *'Nut, spread yourself over your son, Osiris Pepi* [the King], *and conceal him from Seth…*

> *You have encircled for yourself the land and everything within your arms. You have placed for yourself this Pepi as an Imperishable Star that is in you.'*
>
> (*PT* 427, 432; Allen, 2015, p. 108)

The Imperishable Stars were located in the northern sky and were so-called because, with the polar star fixed above the earth's axis, it would neither rise nor set and, because of this, they were considered as everlasting as the Gods (Abd Alrahman, 2020, 25).

This celestial destination persevered through the development of the afterlife realm known as the *Duat* (*dwꜣ.t*), written using the hieroglyph of the five-pointed star. The *Duat* comprised various locations, being a realm that certain Gods traversed on a nightly basis, and where the deceased had to pass through to enter the desired paradise of the *Sekhet-Aaru* or the Field of Reeds *(sḫt-jꜣrw)*. The *Duat* was where the Sun God, Ra, passed through after being consumed by Nut at sunset. In this liminal space Wesir and Ra would merge, becoming a syncretised deity illuminating the realm of the *Duat* (van Dijk, 1986, p. 8). He would pass through the hours of the night, confronting various obstacles until dawn, when he would be reborn in the eastern horizon. Similarly, the dead would need to pass through the paths of the *Duat*, described in the many afterlife books (see below) in order to secure their own rebirth into the afterlife.

In the ancient Egyptian religious view (according to recorded texts), each person possessed a physical body (the *kha*) as well as several spiritual bodies. As is commonly accepted (though not universally agreed upon), preservation of the physical form was apparently vital to the survival of the person and their spiritual bodies. The process of mummification transformed the physical body at death into a *Sah*, thought to be a perfected, purified image that would house the *Ka* and *Ba* when they periodically returned to the tomb (Taylor, 2001, p. 16). The various internal organs were removed and preserved, with the exception of the heart, which was left in place ready for the 'Weighing of the Heart' ritual that took place in the afterlife. The rest of the body was dried in natron salt and wrapped to prevent its decay. The ritual 'Opening of the Mouth' was performed during the funerary rites to re-awaken the deceased, reassembling their spiritual bodies together to fully enter the afterlife. This all related to the first mythic funerary rites performed by Aset and Nebet-het, who recited *sakhu* spells to transform Wesir into an *akh*, rebirthing him into the afterlife and providing an example for the living to follow (Smith, 2017, pp. 129).

The *Ka* and *Ba* were prominent amongst the spiritual bodies, with the former denoting a kind of energetic life-force, and the latter something similar to the individual's personality (Allen, 2015, p. 7). The *Ba* was thought to be the spiritual body that allowed the deceased to move around and engage with the world around them and was often represented travelling as a bird. It is the *Ba* who makes the journey through the *Duat* into the Hall of Two Truths to meet Wesir. Many will be familiar with scenes showing a mummiform Wesir, seated before an oversized set of weighing scales in the Hall of Two Truths. Inpu leads the deceased to present their heart to be weighed against the feather of *ma'at* whereupon, according to *Book of the Dead* spell 30B, the deceased prays that their heart will not betray them. Wesir exercises judgment, often with Aset and Nebet-hut behind him; Ammit (a composite hippopotamus, lion, and crocodile daemon) is ready to consume the heart – and existence – of those whose heart weighs more than the feather; and Djehuty records the results (Taylor, 2001, pp. 37–38).

If accepted by Wesir, the deceased became an *akh*, one of the justified dead (plural *akhu*) who had secured eternal (after-)life. Those who were unsuccessful became a *mut* (plural *mutu*), the angry dead who are sometimes depicted suffering in the less pleasant areas of the *Duat* (Kinsman, 2015). In order to sustain this perpetual existence, the *Ba* would journey back to their tomb to receive offerings from the living, their essence drawn up by the *Ka*. Their *Ren* (name) would also need to recorded somewhere, to ensure the individual's continued existence and memory amongst the living. If their name was forgotten, they could cease to exist (Taylor, 2001, p. 23).

Many tombs – especially those of elite status – contain an area where the living could visit, conduct funerary rituals, leave offerings, and communicate with their deceased relatives. Like the royal mortuary temples, these spaces were designed so that the deceased could continue to receive sustenance in the afterlife, with their *Ka* appearing to receive the offerings left behind. Naturally, as with most burial sites, frequent visits and offerings began to wane over time. To prevent the deceased from going without offerings or being forgotten, their tomb walls and interred goods would represent and list their offerings, and bare the owner's name, so that they might receive the offerings in perpetuity and continue to exist (David, 2018, pp. 15–16). The deceased (and deities) may receive offerings by writing alone – as to write something was to make it real – by depicting it in artworks, or by speaking its existence aloud. This is the intention behind the Offering Formula (see Chapter 6), in which 'voice offerings' are made in addition to, or in the place of the physical offerings themselves.

The Afterlife Books

As time bore on, Egyptian cultural conceptions of the afterlife developed, growing more detailed and demanding more and more rituals and funerary accoutrements. As early as the *Pyramid Texts* it appeared that those who knew the rituals and worshipped Wesir, would gain access to the afterlife:

'As for the one who will truly [worship] Osiris while performing/reciting this magic for him, he will live for ever.'
(*PT Pepi I*, utt. 561B; Smith, 2017, p. 150)

Of course, this knowledge was restricted to those in close proximity to the king and the performance of their rituals. This knowledge widened through the production of the *Coffin Texts* in the Middle Kingdom. These texts were named thus, owing to their location upon coffins; as considerably more people had access to coffins than they did pyramids(!), this made the texts more accessible (though coffins themselves were still expensive to acquire).

Further developments occurred in the New Kingdom, where the *Coffin Texts* moved over to parchment, linen, and other such materials. These are the best known of the ancient Egyptian religious texts (at least by name), perhaps owing to the provocative modern nomenclature of *The Book of the Dead*. Their original name was *The Book of Going Forth by Day*, referring to their aim in assisting the deceased in traveling to and from the *Duat*. As excerpts of this later version of the afterlife liturgies and spells could be inscribed on easily transportable materials and objects, they were more accessible to the Egyptian population than any of their predecessors, allowing more people to gain entry into the afterlife (Ikram, 2003, pp. 39–43). It wasn't just the location of their recording that changed these texts, nor their language over time, but their fundamental ideology as well, from royal celestial ascension, to an afterlife with Wesir for accessible to all (or most).

The Pyramid Texts

The *Pyramid Texts* are the oldest of the ancient Egyptian ritual texts and one of the earliest sources of Wesir's name and mythology. Their sophistication implies that their contents were well-developed prior to their inscription within the royal tombs; however, without textual evidence, their origin – and that of Wesir – remain difficult to concretely determine. As these texts relate to the rebirth of the royal person, Wesir takes a primary role in their content, alongside that of the Creator Sun God. Blending solar and Osirian beliefs, the King would embody the Gods in their journey through the afterlife, to rebirth. As articulated by James Allen:

> *'Osiris himself was envisioned as a mummy lying in the depths of the netherworld, the region through which the sun was thought to pass at night. In the middle of the night the Sun merged with Osiris's body; through this union, the Sun received the power of new life while Osiris was reborn in the Sun.'* (Allen, 2015, p. 8).

According to Allen, the *Pyramid Text* spells (or 'utterances') fall into two categories, ritual and personal, and would be read aloud by a lector priest, likely during the funerary rite; they were also inscribed within the deceased's final resting place so that they continue to echo into eternity (Allen, 2015, pp. 6–7). As is self-explanatory, the ritual spells related to the funerary rituals themselves, aiming to secure the King's afterlife. The Resurrection Ritual appears within the burial chamber and is directed towards separating spirit from matter so that the deceased's spiritual bodies may travel westward toward the Imperishable Stars of the afterlife. Once the funerary rituals were complete, the personal spells came into effect and related to the deceased's individual capacity to travel to and from their tomb. They are personal as they come from the voice of the deceased themselves, written in the first person, in contrast to the second person voice used in the ritual spells, performed for the deceased (Allen, 2015, p. 7).

Offering and 'Insignia' rituals also appear together and denote vital ritual actions performed for the deceased's funerary cult. The former involved making food offerings and libations, ritual cleansing with incense and salt-water, and the performance of the 'Opening of the Mouth' ritual (Allen, 2015, p. 6). The Insignia Ritual involved ritually dressing the deceased's icon. Both sets of rituals involved the 'Reversal of Offerings', whereby, as in later temple cults, offerings were ritually disposed of through eating, drinking, burying, or destroying them. Together, these *Pyramid Text* rituals were essentially the precursors to what would develop into the Daily Temple Ritual (see Chapter 5).

The Coffin Texts

The *Coffin Texts* arise during the Middle Kingdom. Generally, as their name indicates, these are found upon coffins, although they may also appear upon other funerary objects and tomb walls (Hornung, 1999, p. 7). Though some of the *Pyramid Texts* also appear upon coffins at this time, the *Coffin Text* variations are far more common. Significantly, these texts were now available to a wider population, enabling common people to identify as a Wesir. Included within the corpus of the *Coffin Texts* is the *Book of the Two Ways,* preserved in two places. As the title suggests, this book and accompanying vignette visually depict a journey through the *Duat* and the dangers therein, including a 'fiery court' and ferocious knife-wielding guardians (Hornung, 1999, p. 11). Erik Hornung notes that these texts introduce a new funerary motif, that of reuniting with loved ones in the afterlife, though this disappears in the subsequent *Book of the Dead* (Hornung, 1999, pp. 9, 17).

The Book of Coming Forth by Day (The Book of the Dead)

The *Book of the Dead* makes its first appearance at the end of the Middle Kingdom in the 17th Dynasty and become the more popular variation by the New Kingdom (although, again, *Coffin Text* spells continue to make an appearance; Hornung, 1999, p. 7). This afterlife book is predominantly recorded on papyrus, though it also appears in other places and is sometimes written in hieratic script, a form of cursive hieroglyphs, accompanied by illustrations. The *Book of the Dead* is primarily concerned with assisting the deceased in the afterlife, with the Judgement of the Dead (*BD* 125) playing a key role. Obviously this afterlife book, and its intriguing modern name, is the most well-known today.

Other Books

The New Kingdom attests to the presence of numerous other afterlife books. The *Books of What is in the Duat* (referred to today as the *Books of the Netherworld*) were once again restricted to the purview of Egyptian kings, handed down until the 21st Dynasty. These books are primarily concerned with the nocturnal regeneration of the sun and his journey through the underworld (Hornung, 1999, pp. 26–27). One of these books was the *Book of Amduat*, which details the journey of the Sun God through twelve hours of the night, from sunset to dawn. Wesir is depicted and mentioned throughout, though he himself does not speak in the text (Hornung, 1999, pp. 33–34).

Like the *Book of Amduat*, the *Book of Gates*, and the *Book of Caverns* also concern themselves with the hourly journey of the sun at night, though the content of the hours differs. Unlike the other royal netherworld books, the Judgement of the Dead appears in the *Book of Gates*. Located opposite to this book in the Osirieon at Abydos, is the *Book of Caverns*, within which Wesir and Re appear as a single deity (Hornung, 1999, pp. 55, 62, 85). Other royal netherworld books are the *Spell of the Twelve Caves*, the *Book of the Earth*, and various *'Books of the Sky'* (Hornung, 1999, pp. 54, 95, 112–122). In addition to this as non-royal afterlife books, such as the *Books of Breathing* which date to the

Graeco-Roman period, although the earliest is attested from the 30th Dynasty (*c.* 350 BCE). These books claim to have been written by Aset and Wesir (First Book) and Djehuty (Second Book), with the latter only surviving from the Roman Period. Their subject is focused on the importance of the breath and the survival of the name of the deceased in order to remain in the afterlife (Hornung, 1999, pp. 23–24).

A Contemporary Pagan Perspective

There are various books out there discussing modern Pagan conceptions of death and the afterlife, funerary rituals, ancestor veneration, and the practice of 'death midwifery'. Certainly some, though obviously not all, aspects of Egyptian Osirian rituals and beliefs are adaptable to contemporary life. Wesir has a lot to teach us about what comes next, whether we adopt an Egyptian interpretation of the afterlife, or meditate with Wesir in order to meditate on the possibilities.

It is a matter of personal preference whether one decides to participate in ancestor veneration and establish a cult of their *Akhu*, or not. If you have ancestors that you wish to honour and remember, whether relatives, adopted or chosen family, or ancestors of your land or spiritual tradition, it is up to you to decide if an Egyptian approach is appropriate for them. If you feel that your ancestors would not appreciate receiving a Pagan ritual of remembrance, then perhaps a more neutral method would be best, such as lighting a candle in front of their photograph and simply greeting them. If you feel that death moves us beyond religious and cultural boundaries, or that your ancestors would welcome your own approach, then perhaps an Egyptian-style ritual would work well. Plenty of Egyptian Pagans also choose to give offerings to ancient Egyptian ancestors, such as known Pharaohs or officials. There are many options to explore.

Ancestor Shrines

When creating an ancestor shrine, you should think carefully about its positioning, ideally avoiding places in the home where you would not wish for your ancestors to observe the activities that take place there (bathrooms and bedrooms being obvious examples); dining and living areas could be preferable. However, if space is limited, you could consider creating an ancestor shrine within a cupboard that can be opened and closed, or behind a curtain.

Establishing an altar or shrine with their name and/or image is recommended in order to make a clear connection to the person being remembered. *Akhu* shrines can therefore be populated by photos of our ancestors or items inscribed with their names. Other items may include candles, an incense burner, a vessel for liquid offerings, and a bowl or plate for other offerings (see Chapter 4 and fig. 4). According to ancient Egyptian tradition, one must endeavour to keep the shrine as clean as possible, dusting frequently and refreshing offerings.

Rituals to the *Akhu* are founded upon the premise that to depict, recite, or record something is to make it real. Offerings may be represented through image, text, or spoken word, or given in physical form. You may speak the offering formula (provided in Chapter 6) and those offerings will be delivered. Lighting candles and offering incense is an ancient practice that continues into the modern day and lets your beloved dead know that you are thinking of them. Sometimes the ancient Egyptians would write (or commission scribes to write) letters to the dead, asking after them or requesting that they intervene in earthly matters (Troche, 2018, p. 1). The practice of writing letters to the dead likewise continues as a contemporary Pagan practice today, often functioning as prayers letting our deceased loved ones know that we are thinking of them, or sometimes aiming to resolve unfinished business and obtain closure. This is a perfect example of an ancient tradition with continued relevance in the modern day. A practice of which I am particularly drawn to is inscribing a letter or prayers onto a red bowl, which is then used for offerings (Ritner, 2008, p. 182); this could be achieved by creating your own bespoke offering bowl from clay and painting or inking a message onto its surface, or pyrographing a wooden bowl.

As an intermediary between the living and the dead/reborn, Wesir may be appealed to when we wish to commune with our ancestors and beloved *akhu*.

Journeying Between the Worlds

Moving away from the subject of literal death and ancestors, there are further possibilities for the cult of Wesir and his cyclic mythology regarding moving between the worlds. Developed from his PhD thesis in religious studies, Jeremy Naydler's book, *Shamanic Wisdom in the Pyramid Texts* (2005), provides alternative (yet academically informed) readings to mainstream Egyptology, wherein he posits that the *Pyramid Texts* were mystical in nature, conferring 'shamanic wisdom based on the experiences of the living king, thrust into extreme psychological and existential predicaments and perilous encounters with alternate realities' (Naydler, 2005, p. 3). His interpretation of utterance 373 can be used as an example of his argument. The utterance reads:

> *'Raise yourself, Teti! Receive your head, assemble your bones for you, collect your limbs for you, clear away the earth on your flesh for you, receive for you your unmouldering bread and your unrotting beer…*
>
> *Raise yourself, Teti! You have not died.'*
>
> (*PT Teti*, utt. 373; Allen, 2015, p. 87)

Here, King Teti, is told to gather up his limbs and reassemble his body, which – though evocative of Wesir's mythic reconstitution preceding his rebirth into the afterlife – Naydler argues is not wholly dissimilar from metaphorical dis-memberment and re-memberment common within shamanic traditions attested across the globe. Further, as in the example above, the *Pyramid Texts* repeatedly state that the king has not died, 'He lives, this Unas lives! He is not dead, this Unas is not dead!' (utt. 219). This has been consistently interpreted by Egyptologists as referring to the deceased king having risen from death into rebirth in the afterlife. Naydler, however, questions whether the reader should accept what the text is literally saying, that the king is in fact 'not dead', but has actually awoken from a shamanic journey. Indeed, referring back to utterance 373 above, the king is instructed to collect himself and shake the earth (dust) from his body, which (according to Naydler's interpretation) appears more akin to re-emerging from a trance-like state lying upon the ground, rather than a funerary rebirth (Naydler, 2005, p. 61).

There are reasons I am hesitant to support this intriguing reading; for example, the text states that the king should collect his unmoulding bread and beer, which is only possible in the afterlife. Further, the following utterance proclaims that the king has 'become great... bearing your name of Osiris' – identifying with Wesir, rather than the living Heru (*PT* utt. 374). Nevertheless, as a religious studies scholar, Naydler's interpretations throughout the book may ring true to those experienced with shamanic journeying, compared to readings by non-mystically-inclined Egyptologists. It is for this reason that I have included mention of Naydler's work here, for readers who may be interested in exploring shamanic readings of the *Pyramid Texts* for themselves. Indeed, many practitioners are experienced in travelling between the worlds, including those of the living and dead, and so perhaps the Egyptian afterlife books with their maps and directions could be used as guides for such journeys undertaken by the living. I recommend exercising caution and reading up before you try this, for the Books make clear that such journeys are (literally) not for the faint-hearted and are populated with many inhospitable Beings and threats. An experienced Journeyer would know to travel cautiously, in any case.

Chapter 4

Temples & Cults

According to the 1st century BCE Greek author, Diodorus Siculus, Egypt was populated with numerous tombs/temples of Wesir, owing to the myth of his dismemberment:

> *'... Isis recovered all the pieces of the body except the privates, and wishing that the burial-place of her husband should remain secret and yet be honoured by all the inhabitants of Egypt... Over each piece of the body, as the account goes, she fashioned out of spices and wax a human figure about the size of Osiris; then summoning the priests group by group... she said that she was consigning to them alone the burial of the body... It is for this reason that even to this day each group of priests supposes that Osiris lies buried in their district, pays honours to the animals which were originally consecrated to him, and, when these die, renews in the funeral rites for them the mourning for Osiris.'*
>
> (Diodorus Siculus, *Library of History*, 1.21)

This was concurred by Plutarch in the proceeding century, who added that Aset hoped this would confuse Sutekh so that he 'he might despair of ever finding the true tomb when so many were pointed out to him, all of them called the tomb of Osiris.' (Plutarch, *Isis and Osiris*, 18). Wesir's worship was widespread, with temples and shrines attested across Egypt, and his cults spread across the Mediterranean. There is one place in particular, however, where the cult of Wesir had the most profound, long-lasting presence.

Lord of Abydos

Beyond a shadow of a doubt, Abydos was the most important, and oldest, cult centre of Wesir in Egypt. The site was known to the ancient Egyptians as '*Abdjou*', and as '*Ebot*' to the later Egyptian Copts; the name 'Abydos' comes from the Greek translation of the former name (David, 2018, p. 26). The archaeology implies that this site was used for religious purposes since predynastic times through to the 7th century CE, with tombs belonging to the kings predating and comprising the 1st dynasty (*c.* 3100-2890 BCE), and some from the 2nd dynasty (*c.* 2890-2686 BCE) (Oakes, 2006, p. 148). People from far across Egypt of variant social standings sought to be buried in cemeteries surrounding Abydos through to the Ptolemaic period, hoping to be buried in proximity to Egypt's earliest kings and the alleged burial place of Wesir himself.

The earliest deity attributed to Abydos was the jackal-headed God, Khentiamentiu, whose name means 'Foremost of the Westerners' (the Westerners being the blessed dead). At temple of Khentiamentiu was located at Abydos and became syncretised with the cult of Wesir following the 6th Dynasty, before becoming wholly subsumed by the latter by the Middle Kingdom, *c.* 1950 BCE (David, 2018, p. 26).

During the New Kingdom's 19th Dynasty, Abydos became home to one of the most impressive surviving temples in Egypt today – that of Seti I and his son Ramesses II. The temple is dedicated to several deities: Amun, Re-Harakhty, Ptah, Aset, Heru, and, principally, Wesir. It also houses a shrine to the deified King Seti I. Visitors today can enter the Temple, which is still roofed, and visit each of these shrines and admire reliefs depicting the Gods and their barque-shrines (boat-shrines that would carry smaller-scale icons of the Gods, allowing them to 'visit' the temples of other deities during festivals). Each shrine has a relief of a false door, which would allow the deity of that shrine to enter and leave during rituals (David, 2018, pp. 125–126). Wesir's chapel, however, is the only chapel to contain a real door leading to a complex of rooms dedicated to him, Aset, and their son, Heru. As this room effectively acts as the other side of the false door's made manifest, Alison Roberts tantalisingly described this as 'passing into an area normally sealed off from the living. It is as if we are entering directly into the mysterious *Ka*-realm of Osiris' (Roberts, 2000, p. 60). This should certainly be kept in mind for any pilgrims visiting the Temple today!

Significantly, behind the temple is a further structure, known as the Osirion, an alleged burial place of Wesir, now thought to be a 'duplicate tomb' of Seti I (who was actually interred in the Valley of the Kings; Oakes, 2006, pp. 102, 149). Though it is roofless and exposed today, this structure would have been a subterranean, columned chamber holding a faux sarcophagus, presumably representing the burial place of Seti I. Uniquely, the sarcophagus would have been raised in the centre of a channel of water, appearing as an island. Today, the water glows green from algae, reminiscent of the hue of Wesir's skin, adding to the mysterious atmosphere of the place.

Abydos is also home to the royal burial ground Umm el-Qa'ab (أم القعاب), or 'Mother of Pots' (named thus owing to the significant spread of pottery upon its surface). This is the necropolis of Egypt's earliest kings, including the tomb of the 1st Dynasty Djer, which was believed to the tomb of Wesir from the 18th Dynasty onwards (David, 2018, p. 265). This shows how, much like people today, the Egyptians felt a sense of awe towards monuments that were already hundreds of years old, sensing the spirits of the ancestors and the divine who dwelt there.

The temple at Abydos was deserted following the Christian period, having been briefly used as a church (as occurred across numerous ancient Egyptian temples), until 1731 CE, when it was officially recorded as rediscovered beneath the sand (David, 2018, p. 26).

Busiris, Abusir Bana

Another ancient city with a deep connection to Wesir was Abusir, whose Greek name, Busiris, was derived from the ancient

Egyptian meaning 'House of Wesir' (*pr wsr*). Like Abydos, this was the site of royal burials during the Old Kingdom and featured its own pyramids, earlier than the more famous pyramids of Giza (Wilkinson, 2000, p. 121). It is speculated that the important Osirian ritual of 'Erecting the Djed Pillar' originated here (see Chapter 5; David, 2018, p. 273).

Temple of Aset at Philae

Though the island of Philae on the border between Egypt and Lower Nubia housed temples dedicated to several deities, it was principally home to the Temple of Aset. This island was a place of great importance to the cult of Aset and her divine family in the Late Period, especially amongst the Kushite Dynasty, and rose in further prominence during the Graeco-Roman period. Its remoteness, coupled with the devotion of its priests and pilgrims, allowed the Temple of Aset to impressively withstand the conversion to Christianity up until 550 CE, being one of the very last temples to close. Nubian pilgrims left behind their prayers engraved upon the temple's walls up until 456 CE, leaving a lasting testament of their faith in the Osirian triad to still be seen thousands of years later (Ashby, 2019, p. 200).

As can be expected of a place dedicated to Aset, this outstanding temple is also sacred to Wesir and their son Heru. Here, Wesir and his divine family triad were the recipients of Nubian milk libation rituals (see Chapter 5; Ashby, 2019, p. 204). The temple features numerous scenes depicting the mythology of Aset, Wesir, and Heru. A temple vestibule contains reliefs mourning the death of Wesir and his sequential re-memberment. Scenes depicting his rebirth also appear on the gateway leading toward the river, constructed by the Roman Emperor Hadrian; here remains a curious scene of a Nile crocodile bearing Wesir's body to safety on the nearby island of Bigeh (Wilkinson, 2000, pp. 214–215).

Bigeh Island

South of the temple at Philae is the island of Bigeh (Greek Abaton), which from the Graeco-Roman period was believed to be another burial site of Wesir – and in some cases Aset too – and thought (incorrectly) to be the source of the Nile. A temple was located on the eastern side of the island and retained an enigmatic status as the 'forbidden place' where only priests could tread, owing to the Osirian rituals performed there (Wilkinson, 2000, p. 215):

> *'the bodies of these two gods* [Wesir and Aset] *rest, not in Memphis, but on the border between Egypt and Ethiopia, on the island in the Nile which lies near the city which is called Philae, but is referred to because of this burial as the Holy Field…'*
>
> '…[at] *the tomb constructed for Osiris…* [there are] *three hundred and sixty libation bowls which are placed around it; for the priests appointed over these bowls fill them each day with milk, singing all the while a dirge in which they call upon the names of these gods. It is for this reason that travellers are not allowed to set foot on this island.'*
>
> (Diodorus Siculus, *Library of History,* 1.22).

The need for secrecy and privacy makes sense, considering the rituals were recreations of the funerary rites of Wesir, a God with the status of a deceased (divine) king. Every ten days priests would travel upon the barque of Aset, sailing from the Temple of Aset at Philae to the Temple at Bigeh to visit the burial place of Wesir. Here, Wesir would receive funerary rituals and milk libations seeking to revive the god with life-giving liquid (Ashby, 2019, p. 201).

Chapels of Wesir at Karnak

Wesir appears in various other places across Egypt, including sites not predominantly dedicated to his cult. The temple complex of Karnak, located in Luxor is home to an impressive array of temples, chapels, and columned halls, housing the cults of multiple deities and pharaohs. Once known as *Ipet-isut*, meaning 'The Most Select of Places', Karnak was the cult centre of Amun during the New Kingdom (Wilkinson, 2000, 154). In its north-eastern area an Osirion – one of the many tombs of Wesir – was located, with evidence of pilgrims and clergy having left behind corn-mummies for the God's resurrection (Betrò, 2024, p. 8). In addition to this, a number of chapels were constructed between the Libyan 22nd – 26th Dynasties, dedicated to various forms of Wesir. Within these chapels, elite priestesses known as God's Wives are frequently depicted as active within the cults (Coulton et al., 2018, pp. 272–275, 284).

Temple of Aset at Dendera

Dendera is well known for the exquisitely beautiful, well-preserved Graeco-Roman Temple of Hut-herut. Rooms reached from the roof of the main temple comprise chapels dedicated to the mysteries of Wesir, where scenes from his mythology are depicted. At the rear of the temple (in the south-east) is another, dedicated to Aset in which the cult of Wesir also makes an inevitable appearance (Wilkinson, 2000, p. 150).

Temple of Heru at Edfu

As indicated by some of the temples above, Wesir can be found in most temples dedicated to Aset, and sometimes also of their son, Heru. Surrounding the main sanctuary of Heru's temple at Edfu are several chapels dedicated to other gods, including one dedicated to Wesir (Wilkinson, 2000, p. 207). Within this chapel, by its entrance, is a beautiful, raised relief of what appears to be Aset, bearing the horned solar disk atop her head, who wraps her arms around Wesir's (or the king's) shoulders and gazes into his eyes. In this image, Wesir appears reborn, unbound by his mummiform wrappings though sporting the beard that indicates his afterlife condition. The intimacy and love conveyed by this image is one of my favourite depictions of this divine pair (or Aset/Hut-herut and the deceased king, whichever it may be).

Temple of Mandulis at Kalabsha

Further south again, to the island temple of Kalabsha in Nubia, is an incomplete temple built towards the end of Ptolemaic rule in Egypt, dedicated to Heru-Mandulis (a composite Egypto-Nubian deity), Wesir, and Aset (Wilkinson, 2000, p. 218). Like the Temple of Aset at Philae, it was re-located for its preservation following the construction of the Aswan Dam.

Wesir-Dedun at Gebel Barkal, Sudan

Below the fourth Nile cataract in Sudan, close to the ancient Nubian cities of Napata and Meroe, is the Temple of Gebel Barkal (Wilkinson, 2000, p. 233). Here Wesir's name appears inscribed on a re-purposed block, which is the first recorded appearance of a hymn to Wesir in the land of Kush (Petacchi, 2024).

Iseum Campense, Rome, Italy

Rome was home to a Temple and Serapeum dedicated to Isis and Serapis (a syncretism of Wesir and Apis; see below) which was potentially constructed at the close of the 1st century BCE (Versluys, *Aegyptiaca Romana,* p. 354). The Isiac cults went through periods of popularity and imperial support, to proscription and condemnation, which would see this temple opened, closed, and rebuilt several times.

Sanctuary of the Egyptian Gods, Marathon, Greece

Near to the famous Marathon Beach in Greece, is the remains of a temple built within the grounds of an elite family villa in the 2nd century CE (Mazurek, 2018, pp. 628–630). The temple was dedicated to Egyptian deities and harkened back to their Egyptian origins through the structural inclusion of New Kingdom pylons at its entrance and a small-scale pyramid at its centre. Standing at either side of what was once four pylons at each side of the temple now resides replicas of composite Egypto-Greek cult statues (Dekoulakou, 2011a, p. 25 and 2011b, pp. 26–27). At two of the pylons stands a syncretised Isis-Aphrodite (west) and Isis-Demeter (south); a statue of Wesir-Serapis joins them, depicted wearing a traditional Egyptian nemes headdress and kilt. The original statues are housed in the Marathon Museum close by, but the replicas still have a magical feel to them being in the image of these ancient Gods and in their original locations. The Sanctuary is very interesting to visit as a visual example of how the Greeks adopted Egyptian religious beliefs and converted them into their own understanding (not dissimilar to what we do today).

Mortuary Temples

Though not dedicated to Wesir specifically, temples across Egypt make reference to, and include depictions of Wesir, attesting to the historical endurance and importance of his cult and mythology. Mortuary temples are, therefore, common locations where his name can be found, with the deceased seeking to become like Wesir, gaining entry into an eternal afterlife. This is, for example, artistically rendered by the pharaoh Hatshepsut, whose mortuary temple at Deir el-Bahari features a row of statues depicting her in the mummiform iconography of Wesir. Similar Osiride statues are found far south, within the pillared hall of Ramesses II's Great Temple at Abu Simbel, where visitors are impressed by eight, huge mummiform statues of the king adopting the iconography (and therefore power of) Wesir.

Wesir's Association with Other Gods

In ancient Egyptian religion the theology of syncretism allowed for different deities to merge with one another to create a distinct entity who possessed aspects of each being, whilst the original deities simultaneously maintained their own individuality. Such syncretism occurred in order to fulfil a certain need or purpose gained through combined powers. Alternatively, scholars have also explained this as Gods 'inhabiting the being of another for a transitory time (see Hornung, 1996, pp. 91–99).

Already mentioned is Wesir's merging with the cemetery deity, *Khentiamentiu,* whom he eventually subsumed, and with the Sun God whom he temporarily merged with during his funerary journey. Another well attested combination is the funerary deity, Ptah-Sokar-Osiris, who combined the qualities of the creator-craftsman God, Ptah, the Memphite necropolis God, Sokar, and Wesir. Statuettes depicting this syncretised deity became popular in funerary culture from the New Kingdom and Late Period onwards (First, 2009, p. 219), and is most well-known through the proliferation of figurines in the God's composite image.

Wesir and the Apis Bull

The cult of the Apis Bull originated in the 1st Dynasty of the Old Kingdom (Kahl, 2007, p. 59), though it rose to significant esteem in the New Kingdom. In life, the Apis bull came to be associated with the creator-craftsman God Ptah; in death, the bull resided in the domain of Wesir. A single bull would be heralded as the living Apis, where it would be worshipped and cared for, along with its mother, who was associated with Aset. Upon its death, it would be subjected to funerary rituals, mummified, and interred within the Serapeum tomb in Saqqara (Ikram, 2005, p. 6). This aspect of Wesir's veneration was also recorded by Diodorus Siculus, in which he saw a connection between Wesir's agricultural associations and the role of bovines in farming pursuits:

> *'The consecration to Osiris... of the sacred bulls, which are given the names Apis and Mnevis, and [the] worship of them as gods were introduced generally among all the Egyptians, since these animals had, more than any others, rendered aid to those who discovered the fruit of the grain, in connection with both the sowing of the seed and with every agricultural labour from which mankind profits.'*
>
> (Diodorus Siculus, *Library of History*, 1.21.8)

Wesir's association with the Apis bull grew considerably during the Ptolemaic and Graeco-Roman periods, giving way to the veneration of the syncretised deity, Serapis.

As Egypt came into greater contact with the Mediterranean world, especially in the Graeco-Roman period, substantial mutual cultural exchange took place. Egyptians visited and settled abroad, and Greeks and Romans immigrated to, or visited Egypt, each bringing their own Gods and customs with them, as well as adopting local ones. As cults were established outside of Egypt, they naturally took on local traits, assimilating into new cultural and geographic landscapes. Through *interpretation graeca/romana,* the ancient Greeks and Romans re-interpreted foreign deities through their own cultural lens, giving Egyptian Gods and Goddesses Greek or Roman names and associations. At times this resulted in rather superficial matches; for example, Heru was named Apollo because of their shared connection with the sun, but seemingly little else. Others were matched based on more similarities, such as Aset-Isis and Demeter and Ceres, who were all maternal Goddesses who experienced grief and were related to grain production.

Wesir and Serapis

Serapis formed during a period when Egypt was increasingly Hellenised through Macedonian-Egyptian rulers and growing immigration and migration. Though formed from a syncretism of the Egyptian deities Wesir and Apis, Serapis possessed a distinctly Greek character, adopting attributes from Greek deities such as Hades, Asclepius, and Zeus.

The Serapeum of Alexandria, dedicated to Serapis was evocatively described by the Roman solider and historian, Ammianus Marcellinus in the 4th century CE (which, by then, was already hundreds of years old):

> *'There are besides in the city temples pompous with lofty roofs, conspicuous among them the Serapeum, which, though feeble words merely belittle it, yet is so adorned with extensive columned halls, with almost breathing statues, and a great number of other works of art, that next to the Capitolium, with which revered Rome elevates herself to eternity, the whole world beholds nothing more magnificent.'*
>
> (Ammianus Marcellinus, *The History*, 20.16.12)

Little survives of the Serapeum today, though its ruined remains can still be visited and re-imagined by the creative visitor.

Wesir and Dionysus

Owing to his agricultural proclivities, Herodotus equated Wesir with the Greek God of the vine, Dionysus (Herodotus, *Histories*, 2.144-5). In common with Dionysus, Diodorus Siculus recounts that Wesir was believed to have discovered wine and taught viticulture to humankind:

> *'... the discovery of the vine, they say, was made by him near Nysa, and that, having further devised the proper treatment of its fruit, he was the first to drink wine and taught mankind at*

large the culture of the vine and the use of wine, as well as the way to harvest the grape and to store wine.'

(Diodorus Siculus, *Library of History,* 1.15)

Other parallels were made between the two in that they both experienced tragic mythic deaths and rebirths and could, therefore, identify with the human experience of grief (Darby, et al, 1977, p. 165). Diodorus Siculus described Wesir (named Osiris) as, 'laughter-loving and fond of music and the dance', who is always accompanied by musicians, singing maidens (the Muses), and dancing satyrs (Diodorus Siculus, *Library of History,* 1.18); this, however, is more representative of Dionysus' character, than Wesir's, at least according to Egyptian characterisations of their God. Similarly, he states that, 'Some say that Osiris is also represented with the cloak of fawn-skin about his shoulders as imitating the sky spangled with the stars', which is the same dress recorded for Dionysus (Diodorus Siculus, *Library of History,* 1.11.4). This is not evident from native Egyptian sources, although Wesir's association with stars certainly holds up. The same Greek tradition considered Wesir/Osiris and Aset/Isis as symbols of the sun and moon, explaining that the Greek name, 'Osiris', meant 'many eyes', in reference to the rays of the sun (Diodorus Siculus, *Library of History,* 1.11). This solar imagery is corroborated in Graeco-Roman Texts:

'Our Dionysus, shining like a star,
With fiery eye in ev'ry ray'

(Eumolpus, *Bacchic Hymn*; quoted by Diodorus Siculus)

'... the Egyptians called Osiris ('Οσιρις) the Sun. Translated into the Greek dialect 'many-eyed Ósiris,' (one can) see altogether the sun rays as his many eyes all looking upon the earth. But some of the Greeks also called him Sírios by

> *derivation from another name, and another Diónysos... therefore (his name is)... Diónysos.'*
>
> (*Orphic frg.* 237; trans. by James R. Van Kollenburg)

Although Aset received huge popularity (and sometimes controversy) across the Graeco-Roman world through the Isiac cults, Wesir did not receive the same level of veneration in the form of Osiris. More often, his manifestation as Serapis took on the role of Isis's consort, though this was apparently secondary to the worship of Isis herself.

A Contemporary Pagan Perspective

The descriptions of Wesir provided by the Greek sources above, equating him with Dionysus are curious. These images of Wesir are rather different from those that we get from Egyptian sources, though they don't contradict so much as they present new characteristics. Perhaps it is just that the Greeks were describing their own God, Dionysus, and trying to overlay that onto Wesir for their own comprehension (*interpretatio graeca*)? However, if we believe that Gods are living entities, then maybe it is also possible that Wesir showed himself to the Greeks in a different way, presenting as a jovial deity of the vine and the merrymaking that often accompanies its fermented consumption. There are many instances today where contemporary Pagans view deities differently to their ancient counterparts, and this is considered legitimate owing to personal gnosis and the passage of time. If Gods are living entities, then they are capable of developing over time. This potential aspect of Wesir may be worth exploring further, then, to see how he shows up for you individually.

Though many of Wesir's temples have been eradicated or lie in ruins, a number can still be visited today. Modern pilgrimages to sacred sites both share similarities and have stark differences from sacred travel in antiquity. Though travelling to Egypt may not be accessible to everyone today, many individuals may be fortunate enough to embark on a pilgrimage and enter the ancient temples and their inner sanctuaries, which would not have been possible for common people in ancient times. There is no place quite like the Temple of Seti I at Abydos for devotees of Wesir. As the mythic burial place of Wesir (and Egypt's earliest kings) and his primary cult centre, Abydos was a place of pilgrimage to ordinary Egyptians in antiquity, even if they could not enter the temple itself (David, 2018, p. 25). For many, it remains a place of pilgrimage to this day.

Of course, visiting Wesir's sacred sites in Egypt and Nubia would be a powerful experience; however, Wesir can be found much closer to home as well. Ancient Greek and Roman devotees of the cult of Aset marked their temples with Nilometers, representing the Nile flood, though they were a continent apart; devotees also used Nile water (real or symbolic) in their rituals, bringing the Egyptian landscape to their own homeland. Though the Egyptians deeply associated Wesir with their specific geography, devotees abroad found no difficulty in experiencing Wesir and Aset (or Osiris and Isis) at home. It stands to reason that devotees today, living away from Egypt but seeking a connection with Wesir's holy places, could do likewise, recreating symbolic representations of Wesir's sacred sites. As Wesir is de facto Lord of the Dead, it follows that he can be found when walking through cemeteries or known burial sites. One can sense his presence in liminal, watery spaces, at local rivers, springs, or dripping cave mouths. Conversely, he can also be sensed amongst germinating plants in dark soil, ripening fields of wheat, swollen boughs of vineyards. In a modern Pagan context, separated by time, space, and culture, we are creating new cults of Wesir, continuing this long tradition of welcoming Egyptian deities into our local environments.

Making a Home Shrine

In addition to seeking Wesir in natural locations far beyond Egypt and its temples, devotees may also create sacred spaces within their own homes in the form of altars or shrines. Continuing an ancient tradition of household altars into the modern day, devotees today may create shrines within their homes to honour the ancestors and favoured deities, such as Wesir. As mentioned in Chapter 3, when discussing Ancestor Shrines, this should (ideally) be located in a neutral place in the house where the presence of ancestors and deities would be suitable (although sometimes space may limit options). Many Egyptian Pagans today create shrines within a cupboard that can be opened and closed, imitating the opening and closing of the temple's inner sanctuary during ritual hours. Others may use a shelf or table that is permanently accessible. Domestic shrines do not have to be permanent either, if space is limited, or if there is a need for spiritual discretion. So long as the shrine's components and icons are stowed away respectfully in between use, temporary altars can work just fine.

Recent excavations from Tell Edfu, in Egypt's far south, have unveiled a New Kingdom home containing one such domestic shrine:

> *'The shrine was located in a corner of the main room, and traces indicate it was surrounded by a wooden structure. It includes a small fireplace and offering table, two small pedestals in mudbrick, several complete or fragmented stelae (upright inscribed slabs of stone or wood), a rare example of a bust of a female ancestor, and a statuette of a seated scribe.'*
>
> (Lerner, 2019)

Ancient offering tables often had carved representations of offerings onto them, so that they would always be full, regardless of whether or not 'real' items were placed upon them regularly; that way, the ancestor or deity would be in perpetual receipt of offerings.

A domestic shrine today could likewise contain representations of offerings, as well as a bowl, plate, or vessel to hold real offerings. The lighting of lamps and incense is also a commonly occurring practice in ancient Egyptian religion and can be easily replicated today. Home shrines can have a space for candles and incense burners to light as offerings and during rituals. The use of icons and representations is also fundamental to Egyptian religious practice, as to depict something or someone was to make them real and manifest. Modern altars can therefore feature photographs of ancestors and artwork and statues of deities. The addition of various symbols related to the deity may be effective in invoking their presence (see Chapter 6 for symbols of Wesir). Other items may consist of things that remind you of the deity or ancestor, such as special stones, finds from nature, personal trinkets. I always associate Wesir with lapis lazuli (an ancient connection), moss agate (for his earthy aspects), and citrine (for his solar aspects). It may also be a good idea to include a rattle, like a sistrum, for rituals to awaken the deity when offerings are being made (fig. 4).

Photograph of author's past altar dedicated to Wesir

Should you wish to create a shrine dedicated to Wesir and/or your ancestors, it is important to remember that it is a sacred space, designed to receive the deity or ancestor when you call upon them (should they wish to respond!). As such, you should always keep it dust-free and clean, clear away and replenish offerings, and visit on a regular basis. Some spaces may remain inactive in the sense that they are decorative areas of your home that contain divine icons as a representation of your spirituality and their presence in your life. Other places, however, like altars and shrines, ought to be active and invite engagement and care. This is something that I, admittedly, sometimes fall behind on; however, I would still recommend trying to incorporate tending to your shrine and keeping it clean and dust-free. Afterall, most of us would clean and tidy up before an esteemed guest visited our homes.

Wesir as a Multicultural Deity

Over the years I have observed a common reluctance for contemporary Pagans to (at least consciously) engage much with the Hellenised version of the ancient Egyptian deities. This is in part due to an understandable aversion towards adopting practices that may be interpreted through a modern lens as a form of colonialism or cultural appropriation on the part of ancient (and modern) Europeans (or Euro-descendants). This is an extremely sensitive and complicated thing to discuss in relation to the ancient relationship between the countries we now know as Greece, Italy, and Egypt. However, it is undeniable that ancient Egyptian culture deeply influenced the Mediterranean world and vice versa (not to mention that ancient Egypt also took on the role of a colonising Empire at various points in time).

What has become obvious to me is that, though there is this aversion, many Graeco-Roman interpretations, myths, and practices nevertheless infiltrate the way we view many ancient

Egyptian Gods and Goddesses today. This is especially relevant in the case of Aset and Wesir. The mythology we have become familiar with regarding Wesir is considerably influenced by the versions given to us by the likes of Plutarch and Diodorus Siculus. It is clear that many devotees of Aset and Wesir (or Serapis) across the Mediterranean were devout in their faith and were in awe of Egyptian culture (despite perhaps exoticizing or misunderstanding it). Furthermore, deities have the ability to change over time and reveal themselves to their devotees in different ways. Perhaps Wesir became more Dionysian when he travelled to Greece? And perhaps he appears differently again to devotees across the world today? It is therefore important for modern devotees to have a broad understanding of Wesir's multicultural cults, especially as the vast majority of his modern veneration takes place outside of Egypt, revived by non-Egyptians who are likewise in awe of Egypt's amazing history and culture, but otherwise not a part of it.

Chapter 5

Rituals & Festivals

Rituals have been performed for Wesir at least since the God's first appearance in the *Pyramid Texts* and the funerary rituals that they detail, and his rituals continued to be performed and adapted by devotees up to their proscription in the fourth century CE (as far as we know). Such rituals typically follow the theme of invoking Wesir's (and Aset's) restorative power, presenting offerings, and exalting this name. Some rituals took place on an annual basis, according to a festival calendar, whilst others took place daily within the cult temple, chapels, tombs, or private homes.

The Daily Temple Ritual

In ancient Egyptian state religion, the temple priests would enact daily rituals, entering the Gods' sanctuaries, awakening their statues (by summoning their *ka* to reside within cult icons), presenting offerings, clothing their icons, performing purification rites, and reciting complex liturgies. According to Rosalie David, who studied the rituals of the Abydos temple in depth, the common formula for the daily temple ritual, as of the 18th Dynasty, was a combination of the early solar rituals and those belonging to the cult of Wesir, arising as a composite ritual of Heliopolitan origin (David, 2018, p. 128). On the one hand it centred around the concept that the Sun God was reborn with the dawn, received his daily sustenance and purification during the day, and returned to the western horizon at dusk. Cult rituals were performed three times a day to ensure that the deity was well-provided for, in the belief that their icon was inhabited by their *ka*, or spiritual body and so should not go unattended. Such a routine paired well with the cult of Wesir, who underwent funerary rites to re-constitute his body for recurrent rebirth and likewise needed bathing, clothing, and provisions.

Taking place in the Holy of Holies, the temple's inner sanctuary, it was essential that the rituals were carried out by elite priests observing purity stipulations, with purification rites required before each stage of the ritual was enacted with precise liturgies (David, 2018, p. 131). The cult icon would be treated as if the deity was present in the statue throughout the ritual, being purified, dressed, and given offerings. Though there would have been variations over time and place, there are common steps found in the recordings of the daily temple rituals:

1. At sunrise the ritual priests bathed in clean water and natron salt and were purified with the smoke of incense.
2. Prayers were spoken and incense was offered before entering the inner sanctuary. At Abydos it is shown that the priest first offered incense to the Uraeus Goddess who protected the chapel (David, 2018, p. 131).
3. The priest would open the doors of the shrine and awaken the deity within their icon, kissing the ground before them in reverence.
4. Sand was poured upon the ground and the icon was placed upon it to be undressed, cleansed, and reclothed for the day.
5. Offerings would be presented, accompanied by liturgies.
6. The icon would be replaced within its shrine and priest/s would retreat backwards, sweeping away their footprints in the sand and re-sealing the door to the sanctuary.

The midday and dusk rituals would repeat these steps, with some variations.

Whilst there are sources out there to support recreating formal temple rituals in a modern context, the above may be easily adapted to less formal, domestic use. At its essential core, the ritual requires the following steps:

1. Purification through washing in clean water and using salt, followed by fumigation with incense.
2. Speaking prayers to 'open' the space, directing them at protective deities such as the Uraeus Goddess.
3. Open the shrine, show reverence through a gesture such as bowing, and awaken the deity. The use of sistra or rattles is particularly popular – and authentic – for this.
4. Attend to the icon by cleaning it, anointing with oils, and/or dressing it.
5. Present offerings such as incense, libations, bowls of food etc., alongside prayers.
6. Close the shrine, bidding farewell to the deity, extinguishing candles. Some people leave the room backwards (if able) to signify the official end of the ritual.

Milk Libations at Philae

Egyptologist, Solange Ashby, has argued that Nubian priests and pilgrims frequenting the temples at Philae introduced milk libation rituals to the cult of Aset and Wesir there. As the name suggests, the ritual involved pouring the divine milk of Aset, the 'Beautiful Libationer', to rejuvenate Wesir with the liquid of life belonging to the divine Mother. This milk offering could be depicted as being poured by the king from a *hes* vase before the Gods or poured directly onto an offering table to purify its contents (Ashby, 2019, pp. 200–202). Ashby explains that when Wesir received the milk offering it is as Wesir-Wennefer (*wen-nefer* meaning 'goodness of being'), to emphasise his revived condition, thanks to Aset's magic. Indeed, similar milk libations were an essential feature of Nubian funerary rituals seeking to revive the deceased; they are not found elsewhere in Egypt but are attested in multiple Lower Nubian temples. Their importance to Wesir's Nubian devotees is demonstrated through pilgrim inscriptions surrounding these reliefs at Philae, especially during the second and third centuries CE (Ashby, 2019, pp. 202, 204, 206). This makes milk libations one of the latest examples of rituals performed for Wesir, prior to the closure of the temples following the spread of Christianity, which makes them feel all the more special when reviving them in Wesir's veneration today.

Funerary Rites

According to mythology, Wesir was the first to undergo funerary rites and to experience rebirth, with his divine sisters, Aset and Nebet-hut, officiating as the first celebrants and mourners. There are many sources out there providing detailed information on ancient Egyptian funerary rites, typically for the elite or wealthy. Should readers wish to explore this subject further however, for a variety of reasons, their full recreation may not be appropriate, possible, or desirable for modern devotees of Wesir. Nevertheless, the spirit of these rituals and the need for a final farewell, a space for grieving, and a communal opportunity to celebrate a loved one's life, remains.

The mytho-liturgical *Songs* and *Lamentations of Isis and Nephthys* are recorded from the 2nd century BCE, with the former (the longer text) designed for use at the temple at Abydos (*Papyrus Bremner-Rhind*; BM EA10188), and the latter for use in funerals. Overall, these texts recount the mythology of Wesir's demise and act to facilitate his rebirth, and by extension that of the deceased. The following excerpt from the *Songs of Isis and Nephthys* beautifully capture the Goddesses' grief and wish to see their beloved again:

'{Isis sings}
Even as I desire to see you!
I am your sister Isis, the desire of your heart,
Yearning after your love while you are far away;
I flood this land with tears(?) today.

{Duet}
Draw nigh, so please you, to us;
We miss (?) life through lack of you.
Come you in peace, O our Lord, that we may see you,
O Sovereign, come in peace,
Drive trouble (?) from out of our house,
Consort you with us after the manner of a male.

(*Songs of Isis and Nephthys*, 3,15-3,22;
trans. by R. O. Faulkner, 1936, p. 124)

Excerpts and themes from these liturgies could be recited in funerary rites today, joining a timeless, ancient prayer conveying grief – which is an expression of love – for those who have passed on. For some, reclining in the winged embrace of Aset and Nephthys, the first mourners, may be able to offer comfort during such times.

The Wag Festival

Sometime between the 17th–19th days of the first month of the flood season of *Akhet* (Coptic Θωογт, Arabic توت), the festival of *Wagy* was observed (Poo, 2009, p. 149). This celebration was associated with funerary rituals as early as the 4th Dynasty and seems to have involved visiting the tombs of the deceased and presenting them with offerings (El Din Anwar, 2019, p. 8). Owing to its mortuary associations, this would eventually become connected with the growing cult of Wesir. As early as the Pyramid Texts Wesir was said to 'come as Orion, Lord of wine during the Wag-festival' (*PT* 442; trans. by Faulkner,

p. 147), with the drinking of wine becoming a key part of the observances. It is possible that the return of the flood and its cyclical fertility served as a reminder of afterlife resurrection; hence, the combined significance of the festival as one honouring the dead alongside agricultural renewal (Poo, 2009, p. 150).

The Mysteries of Osiris

In the modern Coptic calendar, *Khoiakh* (Coptic Ⲕⲟⲓⲁⲕ, Arabic كياك) typically falls between late December and early January. In antiquity it would have been closer to October and November, dependant on when the inundation arrived to start the New Year. In either case, *Khoiakh* is consistently referred to as the fourth month of the inundation season of *Akhet* and this is the month in which the Mysteries of Osiris were typically observed (Jauhiainen, 2009, pp. 113–114).

The 12th Dynasty stela of Ikhernofret records how he, following instruction from the king and substituting for him, performed the Mysteries of Wesir at Abydos. Ikhernofret performed the role of Heru/the king, son of Wesir, creating a beautiful barque and palanquin to carry Wesir's icon and many treasures towards the temple in Abydos (*Stela of Ikhernofret*, 10–14). Here, he instructed the priesthood of Abydos on how to perform the correct rituals for the Mysteries, with Ikhernofret himself attending to Wesir's cult image: 'I was pure of hand in decorating the god, a *sem*-priest clean of fingers' (emphasising the importance of ritual purity). He then recounts performing a re-enactment of quashing Wesir's foes:

> *'I conducted the procession of Wep-wawet when he proceeds to avenge his Father. I repelled the rebels from the neshmet-barque and I felled the enemies of Osiris. I conducted the great procession following the god at his footsteps. I caused the barque to sail on, with Thoth leading the voyage…'*
> (*Stela of Ikhernofret*, 15–19; Kelly Simpson, 2003, pp. 425–427)

Thus did Ikhernofret sail along the Nile with the sacred barque of Wesir, receiving cheers from people gathered along its banks. In addition to their performance in Abydos, the Temple of Dendera also attests to their enactment, and though dating to the Ptolemaic period, they likely retained much traditional content (David, 2018, p. 266). Though not privy to the rituals of the inner sanctuary, pilgrims would travel to Abydos to join the festivities and the reenactment of the Mysteries, erecting stelae to mark their visit and leaving votive offerings. The plenitude of these offerings, given over centuries, is evidenced by the scattered remains that coat the ground at the aptly named Umm el-Qa'ab (أم القعاب, 'Mother of Pots'), adjacent to the Abydos temple (Roberts, 2000, pp. 48–49).

As part of these festivities, clergy and commoners alike, created corn mummies (described in Chapter 2). Fortunately for us, a text from Dendera provides instructions on their construction and ritual use. Below is a translated and explained guide to this:

1. *'...in Busiris, it is performed there on the fourth month of Inundation, day 12, in the presence of the Shentit...'*
   Busiris was a settlement in the Delta which housed a cult of Wesir. *Shentit* means 'widow', referring to the Goddess, Aset.
2. *'...with 1* hin *Barley and 4* hin *of sand. Put it in a basin.'*
   This basin should be ritually consecrated to protective deities, as indicated below. 1 *hin* is approximately 0.45 litres (i.e. *c.* 280g of Barley and *c.* 2304g sand).
3. *'Pour divine water over it every day, ¾* hin, *from a pitcher of gold and in the presence of the Shentit, while you recite the spells over it regarding the 'Pouring of Water over the Bodily Remains'. The guardians of the basin will protect it until the advent of the fourth month of Inundation, day 21.'*

The mixture should be watered for eight days, presumably evaporating (considering Egypt's heat and the fact that the mixture would otherwise be immersed in a pool of water by the end of the eight days). The spells are not given here, though plenty of examples exist in the afterlife books for pouring sacred water over the body. ¾ *hin* is *c.* 337ml.

4. *'Take it out of the basin and give it the form of a mummy with the White Crown by means of 1* deben *of incense.'*
   This occurs on the morning of the ninth day. This incense would be in its gum form, aiming to make the mixture stick together. The White Crown is the royal crown of Upper Egypt, commonly worn by Wesir in iconography. 1 *deben* is *c.* 91g.
5. *'Tie it with four lengths of papyrus rope, and the basin of the divine remains likewise.'*
   Tie sacred cords around the figure and the bowl (perhaps separately?).
6. *'Allow it to dry by exposing it to the sun for a full day.'*
7. *'Make a water procession with it on the fourth month of Inundation, day 22, on the eighth hour of day.'*
   This takes place on the tenth day, either the eighth hour after sunrise, or 8.00am. A water procession can be interpreted as sailing down the river or in a pool in a sacred barque.
8. *'Let there be many torches around it, together with their guardian gods, Heru, Djehuty, Anpu, Aset, Nebet-hut, the Sons of Heru, and 19 gods. They stand in 34 barques. Dress these gods in four fabrics of the Northern and Southern Mansions.'*
   The procession is accompanied by daytime torchlight, overseen by the gods who have been attended to by their own daily ritual of clothing and sustenance.

9. *'Lay them to rest in the grave, wrapped in the linen of the Khenty-amentiu* [the Foremost of the Westerners] *of the previous year and of the basin of the divine remains likewise. Lay it in a coffin of sycamore wood, with an inscription for Khenty-amentiu in ochre.'*
   The corn mummy and the basin are wrapped in the cloth from the previous year's mummy. The mummy is placed in a miniature coffin bearing the name of Khenty-amentiu, written in ochre (or a rust-coloured) pigment.
10. *'Bury them on the* nebeh-*hill under the sacred persea trees on the last day of the fourth month of Inundation.'*
    As the Egyptian calendrical month consisted of thirty days, the burial takes place on the final day (which would be eight days later). The mummy is buried in a sacred place, though notably *not* a real tomb, but upon a tree-laden hill.
    (*Khoiakh Text*, 18–23; adapted from translation given in Raven, 2012, p. 120)

As corroborated by this ritual process, the festival lasted for eighteen days, starting on the 12th day in the month of *Khoiakh*, and ending on the 30th day, culminating with the ritual raising of the Djed Pillar.

Raising the Djed Pillar

The 19th dynasty Temple of Seti I at Abydos provides illustrated details for the performance of the festival of the Raising of the Djed Pillar (*'sah Djed'*, *sḥ ḏd*) (Oakes, 2006, p. 155). This festival related to the ritual resurrection of Wesir, raising the pillar – that is, his backbone – to an upright position, and it is recorded across several temples (fig. 5). The festival took place at the end of the Mysteries of Wesir, on the 30th day of the month of *Khoiakh*, celebrating Wesir's resurrection and though the ritual raising of the pillar is attested in differing contexts, it consistently represented rebirth and renewal (David, 2018, pp. 272, 274).

The Rising of the Djed Pillar, Temple of Seti I at Abydos
Photograph by Olivia Church, 2017

Festival of the Two Kites

According to the *Bremner-Rhind Papyrus* (1:1-2), the *Festival of the Two Kites* took place between the 22nd and 26th day of the fourth month of the inundation (*Khoiakh*), either coinciding with the *Mysteries of Wesir*, or existing as a variant name for the same festival. It is during this observance that the lamentations and songs of Aset and Nebet-hut were recited:

> *'The entire temple shall be sanctified, and there shall be brought in [two] women pure of body and virgin, with the hair of their bodies removed, their heads adorned with wigs... tambourines in their hands, and their names inscribed on their arms, to wit Isis and Nephthys, and they shall sing from the stanzas of this book in the presence of this god.'*
>
> (*Songs of Isis and Nephthys*, 1,2-1,5; trans by. R. O. Faulkner, 1936, p. 122)

The text above describes how two unmarried women underwent the process of ritual purification and performed the role of the Kite goddesses, Aset and Nephthys, playing music and reciting the Goddesses funerary liturgy for Wesir. This is a significant sacerdotal role to play, embodying the Goddesses and ensuring Wesir's successful rebirth (and therefore all subsequent rebirths in existence).

The Epagomenal Days and Wep Ronpet

At the village of Deir el-Medina, the five epagomenal days leading up to the New Year, *Wep Ronpet*, were known as the 'five days upon the year' (*'heru 5 hery ronpet'*, *hrw 5 ḥry rnpt*), with each day marking the birth of one of Nut's five children. As the heir of his father, Geb, Wesir was the first born on day one (Jauhiainen, 2009, p. 196). Though this was a time of chaotic potential, with the flood causing structural damage and driving vermin (and their diseases) into the settlements, not to mention the extreme summer heat at that time of year, the flood was also essential to agricultural life in Egypt. When the waters retreated again, the Nile Valley was left fertile and ripe for sowing crops. As a deity associated with agriculture and the Nile's depths, Wesir's birth on the first epagomenal day was something to celebrate:

> *'His life-giving power existed in the floodwaters of the annual inundation, which brought renewed vitality to Egypt's agricultural land; in the germination of seeds into living plants; in the growth of an egg or fetus into a living being; and in the Sun's daily rebirth.'*
>
> (Allen, 2015, p. 7)

The flood usually came around the same time as the rise of the north star, Sirius (*Sopdet*, to the Egyptians). In some sources, where Aset is equated with the star, its rising in the heavens was interpreted as Aset taking to the skies to search for the body of Wesir, flooding the land with her tears. As mythic cycles can be non-linear in terms of the calendar year, it would not be a contradiction to concurrently witness Aset's grief as well as celebrating Wesir's birth on the first intercalary day of the year.

The Festival of Lamps (Roman Lychnapsia)

There were various festivals celebrated by the Egyptians, Greeks, and Romans, which principally involved lighting lamps and having lamp-lit processions. One such festival took place on the fourth epagomenal day celebrating the birth of Aset (see above). In the Roman Empire, it took place around 12th August, which likely also corresponded with the epagomenal days (Malaise, 1972, p. 229). Other lamp festivals took place to specifically mourn Wesir, reenacting Aset's search for his body. This seems to have taken place around the 22nd day of *Khoiakh* (Griffins, 1975, p. 183).

A Contemporary Pagan Perspective

The ancient Egyptian festival calendar was, naturally, intrinsically linked to the Egyptian landscape, the agricultural cycle, and the annual inundation of the Nile. As many modern devotees of Wesir do not live in this environment (and Egypt's modern environment has undergone many changes since antiquity), we cannot always accurately and relevantly recreate this. Instead, some may wish to translate Wesir's mythic cycle onto their own landscapes, privileging contemporary significance over historical accuracy – although, as previously shown (see Chapter 4), non-Egyptian devotees in antiquity did likewise, and so the pursuit of 'historical accuracy' is highly nuanced. In any case, this decision lies with the individual devotee.

A proposed modern festival calendar for Wesir unsurprisingly mirrors that of Aset, owing to their shared mythology. The following dates do not necessarily follow a linear mythic narrative, but are placed close to their approximated ancient date, and/or their seasonal appropriateness.

A Festival Calendar for Wesir

Festival: The *Epagomenal Days* and the *Birth of Wesir*
Date: July/August (around the Rise of Sirius in your location, or the time you celebrate the New Year, if preferred).
Purpose: Day 1 marks the birth of Wesir and Day 6 heralds *Wep Ronpet*, the Egyptian New Year.
Rituals: Celebrate by reading the story of the conception and birth of the children of Nut and Geb. Give offerings to the Gods on each of their days of birth, concluding with prayers or spells of protection (as these days were also associated with chaotic forces).

Festival: *The Festival of Lamps (Roman Lychnapsia)*
Date: July/August, 12th August, or December/January.
Purpose: This was a festival celebrated by devotees of Aset, marking the rise of Sirius in the heavens in conjunction with the arrival of the Nile flood. It was also a festival marking Aset's search for the body of Wesir.
Rituals: The *Festival of Lamps* was observed by candlelit processions as devotees imitated Aset seeking the body of her beloved. You can celebrate by carrying out your own candlelit procession searching for Wesir, or by lighting candles in a row and contemplating Aset's grief as she seeks her beloved.

Festival: *The Mysteries of Osiris* and *The Festival of the Two Kites*
Date: October/November
Purpose: To mourn the death Osiris and hold his funeral through sacred drama. This takes place over the course of five days.
Rituals: Celebrate by recreating a ritual drama, enacting the myth of Wesir, his death, funeral, and resurrection. Recite the *Songs* and *Lamentations of Isis and Nephthys*, and take time to remember, give offerings, and light candles to your own *akhu*.

Festival: *Raising the Djed Pillar*
Date: October/November (four days after the end of the *Mysteries*); alternatively, the Spring Equinox, when balance is restored and the return of life is observable.
Purpose: To raise the Djed Pillar and celebrate Wesir's rebirth, following his funerary rites.
Rituals: Celebrate by raising your own Djed Pillar in the form of a post, pole, an artistic recreation, or statue of

Wesir himself. Raise the pillar with intention, reverence and music. Gives offerings and celebrate!

Offering Rituals

Though there are many ways one could create and recreate rituals dedicated to Wesir and the Gods of ancient Egypt, it is important to remember that the surviving ritual liturgies we have typically come from formal state religion, rather than the devotional activities of common people. However, should one wish to reconstruct these rituals, I recommend *Eternal Egypt* by Richard Reidy, who went to great lengths of research to recreate liturgies for contemporary use. Alternatively, for those wishing to carry out daily devotional rituals in a more domestic, rather than formal temple context, one may choose to 'open' their shrine with purifying incense and prayers; recite an awakening prayer or invocation, such as, 'Awake... in peace! May your awakening be peaceful!' (Meeks and Favard-Meeks et al. 1999, p. 127); present offerings and leave them there for at least 15 minutes; reverse the offerings (burn, discard, or consume); and then purify the shrine before closing it and withdrawing from the space backwards (if possible).

The offering ritual is the most common ritual you can do for an Egyptian deity or ancestral spirit. Though belonging to the 18th–19th Dynasty *Ancestor Ritual* from Abydos, aimed at reviving and offering to the ancestral king/s, the contents of the following excerpt seem appropriate for use in an offering ritual to Wesir, who is, after all, the very first Divine ancestor.

'Wash your hands,
Open your mouth, unstop your ears.
See with your eyes, speak with your mouth...
Come to this your bread that is warm
and to this your beer that is warm...

Enter into this your bread,
And to these your divine offerings,
In your place and in your temple
For ever and ever.'

(Roberts, 2000, p. 76)

One could also choose to speak the traditional offering formula in their own language and/or approximated ancient Egyptian. The example below has been slightly edited, with *nisu* ('King') replaced with *shemsu,* ('follower'), as modern devotees usually make offerings on behalf of themselves, rather than a monarch. I have also inserted Wesir's name and epithets:

'hotep di shemsu
An offering which the follower gives (to)

Wesir, knenty-amentiu, nb Abyjoo
Wesir, Foremost of the Westerners, Lord of Abydos

di-ef / di-es peret-kheru ___, ___, ___
So that he / she may give a voice offering (of) ___, ___, ___ [offerings]

nebet neferet wabet ankhet netjer eem
Everything good and pure on which a God lives

En ka hen eemakhoo ___.
For the *ka* of the revered one ___ [God or ancestor's name].'

Note that the Egyptian does not provide a neutral gender pronoun in the grammar of this section, though the masculine (*dj=f, 'di-ef'* can be used generically). Suggested authentic offerings that could be inserted into line three are as follows (again, appearing in their approximated pronunciation for ease):

akhet = flame
dua = praise
et = bread
henkhet = beer
hetpet = offerings
hesi = to sing/make music
irep = wine
merhet = oil
moo = water
senetjer = incense
irechet = milk

Repeating variations of the offering formula is a magical act. According to ancient tradition, this can just be a 'voice offering' where no physical offerings are required, as by speaking their name, their existence they become real. This means that you could make voice offerings to deities and ancestors just by speaking the prayer before their image, or using their name only, at your altar, in a sacred place, or even in a museum. In fact, a museum close to my home has an information board with the formula written out in Egyptian hieroglyphs, with English and Welsh translations, inviting visitors to do just that! Though creating new prayers from the heart is certainly effective, repeating prayers that have been spoken by thousands of others, across time and geography, can add to their power and allow us to partake in a truly ancient ritual together.

Chapter 6

Magic & Prayers

A great deal of magical texts and paraphernalia has survived from the expanse of ancient Egyptian civilisation, giving us a fairly good idea of how magic was practised by magical specialists and common people. Surviving texts and material culture make it abundantly clear that the practice of magic was prevalent throughout Egypt's history and across the social strata. It appears that some magical workings could be achieved by oneself, although perhaps more commonly a specialist was hired to provide a spell and/or to perform it. Such professional magicians were often priests or learned individuals referred to as *rekh-khet* (*rḫ-ḫ.t*, 'knower of things') (Ritner, 2008, pp. 229–230). This is in part because many spells relied on the combination of written and spoken word and at most periods the general population could not read or write. However, magic could also be harnessed through symbols, objects, ingredients, and actions, without needing to recite the written word.

Magic, or more accurately *heka* (*ḥkꜣ*), was a part of Egyptian temple and domestic religion, embedded within daily life and appearing in the written record from the Old Kingdom through to the Coptic period (Zinn, 2013, p. 4227). In one 10th Dynasty royal text, *heka* is cited amongst a list of the ways that an unnamed creator deity has benefitted humanity:

> '*He made for them magic* [*ḥkꜣ*] *as weapons*
> *To ward off the blow of events*'
> (*Instructions of Merikare*; trans. by Lichtheim, 1973, p. 106)

Most spells and magical tools that survive today reveal that they were primarily (and unsurprisingly) concerned with survival: the survival or mothers and babies during pregnancy, birth, and infancy, healing from illness or poisonous bites, or protection from malignant entities. *Heka* could also be used to attract positive things, as a force inherent within nature that could be harnessed according to one's will. There are hundreds of examples of *heka* used as a protective method by people in real life, as well as by Gods in mythic narratives. As a deity popular amongst clergy and common people, Wesir was often a part of the magical practices to support the needs of daily life, in addition to the transformative magic that took place during funerary rites.

Symbols

Recalling the principle that to depict something made it real and manifest, utilising symbols of Wesir is a simple and effective way to invoke his influence. Helpfully, Wesir is a deity with a very strong iconographic repertoire of recognisable, magically potent symbols. The crook and flail that typically appear in Wesir's crossed arms are clear examples of this. These two items appear as symbols of royalty before they became associated with Wesir, and so his adoption of them firmly aligned him with Egyptian kingship (Smith, 2017, p. 112). Today, the crook can be interpreted to signify Wesir's guiding presence as the shepherd of his devotees; the flail may represent his role as the dispenser or justice and Judge of the Afterlife. In contemporary ceremonial magic and traditional Wiccan ceremonies, the crook and flail (or scourge) may be used by initiates to represent the duality of mercy and severity (Farrar and Farrar, 1984, p. 257) which, though modern, remains relevant to Wesir's nature.

Another important symbol of Wesir mentioned in the previous chapter is the Djed Pillar. This was originally a symbol of the syncretised God, Ptah-Sokar, however, by the New Kingdom the Djed Pillar became synonymous with the backbone of Wesir (Oakes, 2006, p. 155). The word *djed* (when written with the ideogram hieroglyph of the pillar) meant 'stability', perhaps evoking the strength of Wesir's upright body (spine) upon his resurrection.

Hieroglyphic script was known as the *djed medu* (*ḏd md.w*) 'words spoken' (*djed* is spelt differently in this context), indicating that its very purpose was to be read aloud. It was imbued with magic owing to the belief that to write, depict, or speak something was to make it manifest. The name of Wesir in his traditional orthography, therefore, has the ability to manifest his being into existence (see fig. 2). Other symbols and amulets which were utilised in funerary rites, such as heart scarabs or the healing Eye of Heru, may also be used in conjunction with Wesir's veneration today. Calling upon his regenerative aspect, sheaves of wheat and grape vines can be used as symbols of Wesir and his ability for agricultural growth and renewal.

Though not a symbol, as such, the constellation of Orion was associated with Wesir (or the God, Sah) from as early as the *Pyramid Texts*:

> *'"Look, he is come as Orion," (says the Dual Ennead), "as Osiris come as Orion..."*
>
> *... The sky conceives you with Orion, the morning-star gives you birth with Orion. Live! Live, as the gods have commanded you live. You ever go up with Orion in the eastern arm of sky, you ever go down with Orion in the western arm of the sky.'*
>
> (*PT, Pepi I*, utt. 442; Allen, 2015, p. 112).

This constellation appears in the night sky between January and February and is most readily identifiable from the band of three stars comprising 'Orion's Belt'. As Orion appears in the sky in the winter months during the season of death (in the Northern Hemisphere, see Chapter 5), I have always seen its appearance as a sign of Wesir, watching over us as from the other side.

Indeed, it was to this constellation that deceased pharaohs were believed to travel, to unite with Wesir (Wilkinson, 2003, p. 127). For this reason, the five-pointed star of Nut, which decorated temple and tomb ceilings and the interior of coffins, can also be used in association with Wesir, representing his celestial dwelling place.

Ancient Spells

Most spells involving Wesir are funerary in nature (such as the original spells known as the *Pyramid Texts*) and, as such, may not be particularly useful for most readers. As the following ancient spells are removed from their original context, translated in an archaic tongue, and make references to obscure religious concepts, they are included here more for interest than for direct re-use (although readers may find in them the potential for modern adaptation).

Shabti Spells

Though not directly invoking Wesir, the following spell to enchant an ushabti or shabti (*wšbtj* or *šꜣb.tj*) may be of interest to modern devotees. The name 'shabti' derives from the verb 'to answer' and reflects the role of these figurines in responding to the requests of their (deceased) owner. The shabti formula comes from *Coffin Text* spell 472 and Chapter 6 of the *Book of the Dead*, and aimed to instruct 'shabtis to do work for their owner in the realm of the dead'. Depending on one's afterlife beliefs, this could likewise apply today; however, the spell and/or concept could also be adapted to enchant similar figurines to perform tasks for the owner in their spiritual life and in other spiritual realms (depending on one's belief in the ability to astrally travel).

The first version below is a translation of the *Coffin Text* spell, with some minor edits for clarity. The second example is an *edited* version of the spell, written in a more user-friendly way for modern purposes. The third version is a transliteration, suggested pronunciation, and translation of the *Book of the Dead* spell, inviting readers to speak the spell in approximated Egyptian.

The Coffin Text Shabti Spell

Words to be spoken over the image of the owner, preferably on wood, and placed within their chapel:

> *'O you shabtis which have been made for* [Name]*: if* [Name] *be prescribed a task or if an unpleasant duty is imposed upon* [Name] *... You shall say, "Here we are!" If* [Name] *be required to keep an eye on those who work there at turning over new fields, to plant the riparian lands, or to move sand to the West which was placed on the East* [1] *— and vice versa — "Here we are" you shall say in response.'*
>
> (*CT* 472; text adapted from Faulkner, 1977)

[1] This refers to a belief that the afterlife appeared as an idealised version of life on earth (in Egypt) and so contained fields that needed to be worked (see Chapter 3). Shabtis – manifest as afterlife servants – would be given this laborious task, leaving the deceased to enjoy their afterlife in leisure.

The Coffin Text Shabti Spell (Adapted)

Words to be spoken over the image of the owner and placed upon an altar or area reserved for magical workings:

> *'O you shabtis which have been made for me: if I am prescribed a task that I do not desire to do, cannot fulfil, or need you to do for me, may you say, "Here we are!" in response to my delegating the task to you. If I need for you to be my eyes and ears in a situation that I cannot attend to, whether it be in this world or another, may you say, "Here we are," in response to my delegating the task to you.'*

The Book of the Dead Shabti Spell

As Egyptian words carried inherent *heka* within them, it is worth pronouncing them to add extra power to the spell. The first line is the transliteration; the second line in parentheses is the approximated pronunciation; the third line is a translation. 'N' is where to insert the relevant name; for magical work, pronouns can remain the same as in the text as this didn't always matter in their ancient use (but they can be altered in the English if one prefers):

i šwb.ty ipn
(*ee shabti eepen*)
'O shabti figure(s)

ir ip.tw N r irt kꜣt nb.t irr.t im m ẖrt-ntr
(*ir eeptu N er iret ka't nebet ireret eem em kheret-netjer*)
If N is called up to do any work that is done there in the underworld

ist ḥw n.f sdbw im
(*iset hu en-ef sedbu eem*)
Then the checkmarks (on the work list) are struck for him there

r s r ẖrt.f
(*er es er kheret-eff*)
As for a man for his (work service) duty

ip.tw r.k r nw nb ir.tw im.f
(*eep too er-ek er nu neb eer-tu eem-ef*)
Be counted yourself at any time that might be done

r srwd sḫt r smḥt wdbw
(*er serwed sekhet er semhet wedbu*)
To cultivate the marsh, to irrigate the riverbank fields

r ẖnt sa r imnt iꜣbt
(er khenet sa er iment iabet)
To ferry sand to west or east

iry.i mk wi kꜣ.k
(iry-ee mek wee ka-ek)
"I am doing it, see, I am here," you are to say.'

(*BD* Chapter 6; UCL, *Book of the Dead* 6)

Spell against haunting (specifically through nightmares)

This spell refers to the four spirits who guard and protect Wesir in the afterlife and invokes them to protect the living. It was believed that spiritual entities could haunt a person through their dreams and cause real-world negative effects. The following spell specifically uses the words *mut* (*mwt*), referring to the unjustified or corrupted dead who have been denied access to the afterlife, and *djay* (*ḏꜣy*), a daemonic opponent. It can used to ward against such nocturnal hauntings today:

> *'Oh you four glorious spirits there whose function is to keep watch over Osiris! As for the watch you have kept over Osiris, you should act in a similar way with regard to* [victim's name] *born of* [parents' names][1] – *to prevent any male dead, any female dead, and any male opponent or any female opponent which is anywhere in the body of* [name] *from killing him* [2].'

(*Papyrus Chester Beatty VI*, vs. 2, 5–9;
trans. by Borghouts, 1978, spell 8, p. 4)

[1] For modern use, this could be substituted for other familial or close personal connections, if preferred.
[2] The pronoun can be altered accordingly.

The spell concludes with the word for 'spirit' (*ʾḫ*) repeated four times, with four being a traditional number for Wesir's guardians (Borghouts, 1978, p. 100).

Spell to protect against plague or disease

The following spell appears to have been used to ward against the spread of plague. It calls upon the assistance of Wesir, alongside the feline Goddesses of healing and illness, Sekhmet, Bastet, and the serpentine funerary deity Nehebkau. Today the spell should, of course, be accompanied by preventative measures advised by modern medicine, and should not be used as an attempted cure:

> *'Rejoicing and jubilation! Don't take this heart of mine away, this breast of mine for Sekhmet! Don't you take my liver away for Osiris! Don't even let the hidden things that are inside Pe come to an end, on the morning of the counting of the Eye of Horus* [1] *... in the temple. Oh every male spirit, every female spirit, every male dead, every female dead* [2] *– an appearance of any animal, someone whom a crocodile has snatched, who may sneak has bitten, who has died by a knife, who was passed away on his bed – oh murderers belonging to those who are in the retinue of the year and its addendum* [3]*!*
>
> *Horus, sprout of Sekhmet <place yourself behind my> flesh, that it may be kept whole for life!*
>
> *Words to be said over Sekhmet, Bastet, or Osiris and Nehebkau, drawn in myrrh on a bandage of fine linen. To be a placed to a man's* [4] *throat, <in order> not to let an incubus enter him on account of the Beautiful One, or a green-beast* [5] *jump up to me. The life protection of Neith is behind me and before me. The fire spewing of Bastet will fail against the house of a man. A man will say this spell with bunches of fresh plants.'*

(*Papyrus Edwin Smith* [53] 19, 2–14;
trans. by Borghouts, 1978, spell 18, p. 16)

[1] Pe was an ancient Egyptian town in Lower Egypt, known for the veneration of Heru. 'Counting the Eye of Horus' may refer to a festival involving healing the pieces of Heru's Eye, following his battles with Sutekh, Wesir's murderer.
[2] As with the spell above, 'every male dead, every female dead' refer to the unjustified dead (*mwt*); however, this spell also includes malcontent *akh* (*ꜣḫ*) – justified dead – who may be displeased with the living and wish to cause harm.
[3] This list refers to people who have died under unpleasant circumstances; the final sentence here refers to daemonic entities who wreak havoc at the close of the Egyptian New Year.
[4] The pronouns in this spell can be altered accordingly.
[5] Borghouts interprets this as a type of goose – apparently an aggressive one!

Spell to protect against poison (snake bites)

Though the following spell addresses the poison of snake bites – something that remains a risk for many today – it can also be adapted as a protective spell for other bites, a healing spell for burns, or for metaphorical poisons (again alongside professional medical attention).

> *'Oh Re, of Geb, oh Nut, oh Osiris, oh Horus – may you keep firm the heart of this man who suffers! May you restore him to life – as you restored the heart of Re to life during the attack of Grim-Face* [1]*! May you repel the poison that is in his body like he repelled the efflux of Apep that was in the body of the great god. Re is Your protection* [2]*!'*
>
> (*Papyrus Bremner-Rhind* [10] 71-2;
> trans. by Borghouts, 1978, spell 146, pp. 96–97)

[1] A reference to the chaos serpent, Apep.
[2] In one myth the Goddess, Aset, tricks the Sun God, Ra, into revealing his true name – a source of his power – by placing a

serpent in his path. Aset healed Ra in exchange for his name, and so the recipient of this spell can likewise be healed.

An Ancient Divination Method

This divination method appears in a letter 'concerning bowl divination' from the Graeco-Roman period (collated in a volume known as the *Greek Magical Papyri*, or *PGM*) and mentions Wesir as an appropriate deity to call upon for answers. The description below is a section of the longer text, and it ends by prescribing a protective charm in the form of an inscribed silver leaf worn on a cord (from the hide of a donkey – but perhaps leather or a natural material would suffice today instead!):

> *'Inquiry of bold divination and necromancy: whenever you want to inquire about matters, take a bronze vessel, either a bowl or a saucer, whatever kind you wish. Pour water: rainwater if you are calling upon heavenly gods, seawater if gods of the earth, river water if Osiris or Sarapis, spring water if the dead. Holding the vessel on your knees, pour out green olive oil, bend over the vessel and speak the prescribed spell. And address whatever God you want and ask about whatever you wish, and he will reply to you and tell you about anything. And if he has spoken dismiss him with the spell of dismissal, and you who have used this spell will be amazed.*
>
> *The spell spoken over the vessel is:* [1] *... hither to me, O NN* [2] *god; appear to me this very hour and do not frighten my eyes. Hither to me, O NN* [3] *god, be attentive to me because* [*I wish and command this*][4].'
>
> (*PGM IV*, 222–239; trans. by Jackson P. Hershell & Edward N. O'Neil in Dieter Betz, ed., 1986, p. 42)

[1] Greek words beginning this spoken spell have been removed here, but can be found in Dieter Betz, 1986, p. 42).

[2] Insert the name of the relevant God (i.e. Wesir) or deceased person (*akh*) in the place of 'NN'.
[3] As above.
[4] Greek words have again been removed for ease.

Ancient Prayers

Provided below are two translated ancient hymns to Wesir, allowing modern devotees to establish a connection between Wesir's ancient cults and devotees and themselves in the modern day.

Hymn to Wesir

The following hymn to Wesir originated as an early festival liturgy at Abydos but came to be used in funerary contexts, inscribed upon at least five funerary stelae from the 12th and 13th Dynasties, and at least another eight later sources.

'Hail to you, Osiris son of Nut;
lord of two horns, high of crown;
given the Great Crown;
joyful before the ennead;
for whom Atum fashioned reverence
in the hearts of men and gods,
the blessed spirits and the dead;

given rulership in On;
great of forms in Busiris;
lord of fear in the Two Mounds;
great of dread in Restau;
lord of reverence in Heracleopolis;
lord of power in Tenenet;
great of love upon earth;
lord of fair repute in the palace of the god;

great of appearances in Abydos;

given truth of voice before the entire ennead;
for whom slaughter was made
in the great Hall which is in Herwer;
whom the great powers dread;
for whom the great ones rise from their mats;
fear of whom Shu has caused;
reverence of whom Tefnut has created;
to whom the two Shrines of North and South come,
bowing down, so great is fear of him,
so strong is reverence of him.

This is Osiris! Sovereign of the gods;
great power of heaven;
ruler of the living;
king of those yonder;

whom thousands bless in Kheraha;
for whom the sunfolk rejoice in On;
lord of choice offerings in the Upper Houses;
for whom butchery is done in Memphis;
for whom the Night Offerings are done in Letopolis;
for whom the gods see,
and give him praises;
whom the blessed dead see,
and make jubilation for him;
for whom multitudes have mourned in Abydos;
for whom those in the Netherworld rejoice.

Your son Horus has said: "I have come,
having smitten for you those who smote!"'

(*Hymn to Osiris*; trans. by Parkinson, 1991, pp. 118–120)

Horemheb Hymn to Wesir

The following abbreviated hymn is partially recorded in the statue room of the 19th Dynasty tomb of Horemheb:

'Hail to you, Wesir, Lord of Eternity,
Great Mighty One, Foremost of the West,
Perfect King of Everlastingness,
Great of Terror in the Hau-nebut [1] ...
Who removes evil,
Tatenen [2],
Founder of the Shores,
August Djed, Who rules over eternity...
... Fully equipped with body and atef-crown,
Ram-Headed One, Surrounded with uraei...
... Who took possession of the Two Lands when he was still in the womb of Nut,
Who became ruler of the plains of the Silent Land,
Golden of Body, Lapis lazuli-like of the head, turquoise being upon his arms,
Pillar of Heh, Wide of Breast,
Kindly of Countenance, Who is in the Sacred Land,
Heir of Geb, Gracious upon his throne in the seclusion of Naref [3],
Lord of a fair remembrance of him in the palace,
Great of Appearances in the Chapel of the Phoenix,
Ba of eternity, Akh of everlastingness,
Who administers justice in the Netherworld,
Beautiful Orion who crosses heaven...
... Who is carried in pregnancy to the womb of Nut by day and born in profound darkness by night...'
(*Hymn to Osiris*, Tomb of Horemheb; van Dijk, 1986, p. 63)

[1] Possibly the Phoenician coast, or a mythical reference.

[2] Wesir is equated here with another God.
[3] The necropolis of Herakleopolis (van Dijk, 1986, pp. 64, 67).

Modern Prayers

Provided below are some modern prayers dedicated to Wesir or relevant to his cult in the modern day.

Prayer for the Ancestors

'Hail to you Wesir, foremost of the Westerners,
Lord of the Duat, protector of the blessed Ancestors!
May you open your ears to my prayer,
May you open your eyes to my gestures of propitiation,
May you receive my words and allow them entry to the Field of Reeds,
so that they may reach my Ancestors:

Beloved Ancestors, True of Voice (ma'a kheru), Revered Ones (imakhu),
I speak your names with remembrance and love:
[Recite their names]

I wish for you great happiness in your dwelling place.
I wish for you eternal sustenance, peace, and wisdom.
I thank those of you who watch over me,
who have been guides and wards, teachers, and allies.
I remember and speak your names, so that you may live.

Hail to you, ancestors amongst the Imperishable Stars, within the Field of Reeds, and wherever else you may reside!
And hail to the Great God Wesir, who watches over us all!'

Prayer for Strength

'Hail to Wesir, Eternal God Who resides within the Duat, Strong in Life!

May you rise up,
Strong of Back,
Green and virile,
A pillar of Strength,
The Djed Pillar Who Rises in the East after his journey West.

May you rise within me.
May I rise within you.
Lend me your strength and groundedness,
So that I may stand firm, like the stable earth of your father Geb,
Like the upright pillar of your backbone, rising to face the sun above.'

A Prayer for the Tims of Grief

'I speak your name, Wesir, Lord of Life and Lord of the Duat.
Please hear me as I reach out towards you.
Please stand behind me as a pillar of strength,
and comfort me in my time of need,
as your two sisters comforted you
and as their love lifted you up from inertness.

I speak your name Aset, Great of Magic and Queen of Heaven,
Please hear me as I call to you.
Please wrap your wings around me
and fill me with your grace
and healing magic in my time of need,
for you, also, know the pangs of grief and love.

I speak your name Nebet-hut, Hidden One and Divine Screecher.
Please hear me as I shed my tears with you.
Please touch the earth beside me
and hold me in your arms,

and help me to find peace in my sorrow
as you and your sister found peace and love eternal.'

Epithets of Wesir

Epithets function as names or titles belonging to the Gods which typically describe a particular quality of role (Budde, 2011, pp. 1, 3). As such, when one wants to appeal to a God's specific attribute, power, or mood, calling them by their epithet would be most effective, especially when that epithet is spoken in ancient Egyptian. The following is a list of some of the many attested epithets afforded to Wesir in antiquity.

Khenti-amentiu (*ḫnty ʾjmenty.w*, 'Foremost of the Westerners')

Khenti-Duat (*ḫnty-dwꜣt*, 'Foremost in the underworld' (Smith, 2017, p. 315)

Khenti-keku (*ḫnty kkw* 'Foremost in his darkness' (Uranić, 2018, p. 30; Smith, 2017, p. 315)

Neb-Abydju (*nb-ꜣbḏw*, 'Lord of Abydos')

Neb-ankh (*nb-ʿnḫ*, 'Lord of Life')

Neb-Djedw (*ḫnty ḏdw*, 'Lord of Busiris')

Neb-Imenti (*nb-ʾjmenty*, 'Lord of the West')

Neb-neheh, hekah-djet (*nb-nḥḥ, ḥqꜣ-ḏt*, 'Master of the course of time')

Neb-seger (*nb sgr*, 'Lord of Silence')

Res-oodja (*rs-wḏꜣ*, 'Who wakes up complete')

Sekhem wer (*sḫm wr*, 'Great of Power')

Shefy-ty tep (*šfy.ty tp*, 'Ram-headed one' / 'The one whose head inspires awe') (Smith, 2017, pp. 331–332; van Dijk, 1986, p. 9)

Wennefer (*wn-nfr*, 'The One Who Remains Perfect')

Weredj-eeb (*wrḏ-jb*, 'Weary of heart') (*CT* 74; Brotto, 2015, p. 100)

Wesir pa-shed-hemef en Duat (*wsjr pꜣ- šd- ḥm=f n dwꜣt*, 'Wesir who saves his servant in the Underworld') Coulton et al., 2018, pp. 276–277)

A Contemporary Pagan Perspective

Not all devotees of Wesir and Egyptian deities will wish to practise magic, and this introductory book has not attempted to delve into the subject in great detail. However, it was a concept deeply embedded into ancient Egyptian daily and religious life. The Gods each possessed and exerted their own *heka* and so it was beneficial to know how to evade unwanted influences – or know someone who did!

As I described in the previous chapter, there is power in reciting prayers and liturgies that have been recounted by thousands of others across time and place, especially if you can do so in the original language. It is, therefore, worth having ancient prayers in your ritual arsenal; however, modern prayers are just as worthy offerings to the Gods as ancient ones, especially those you can write yourself or compose on the spot. Your words are your offerings, and when they carry personal truth and meaning it is a valuable thing to give to a deity whose worship was suppressed for over a thousand years.

This chapter has endeavoured to provide a balance of cited ancient examples as well as explained adaptations so that readers can access the historical rituals and spells, whilst also having the option to create new versions that work for contemporary practices today.

Conclusion

Worshipping Wesir Today

As I have hopefully articulated throughout the course of this introductory book, Wesir remains a deeply significant deity for veneration in the modern day, despite the vast distances in time and geography from the origins of his cult in the ancient Nile Valley.

There are a multitude of beliefs and interpretations regarding what happens after life and how we can or should to interact with it; the beliefs of some today may echo those once held in ancient Egypt, as well as differ and conflict in significant ways. Regardless, Wesir represents a timeless aspect of the human experience: the grief that comes at the end of our loved ones' lives, and the anticipation of the end of our own. Cultures around the world today have vastly different relationships with death and the dead, from those who regularly interact with the physical realities of the postmortem body, or who welcome their ancestors home during lavish celebrations; to those for whom death is taboo and something to be concealed and kept mysterious and solemn. We all approach this subject in our own way, and it is not always easy.

At the time of writing this, I remain objectively inexperienced with the subject, and so cannot divulge great wisdom relating to it – though I know many other authors and Pagans who perhaps can (Kristoffer Hughes of the Anglesey Druid Order springs to my mind immediately). In any case, a deity like Wesir is timeless in his representation of this infallible fact of life on this earth. Though this subject brings about intense emotions and memories for many, Wesir's omnipresence in this arena can be a profound comfort to some. As the Egyptians observed, and continue to observe, life sprouts from the richness of the earth, nurtured by a combination of the golden rays of the sun, the life-giving substance of water, and the nutrients of dark soil. The plants recede according to their seasonal tides and return to the earth in some way or another, only to return once again. This cyclical pattern of nature tells us that just as death is a fact of life, so too is life's return. To me personally, I interpret this as a tangible sign of Wesir's manifest reality.

When the ancient Egyptians performed their funerary rites, they saw a parallel between Wesir and their deceased loved one/s. As they mourned their passing, they were joined by the divine sisters, Aset and Nebet-hut, who cradled them between their wings as they grieved their loss. Aset took the spark of life residing in her lover's body and grew a new life in his place in the form of Heru. In both Wesir's resurrection into the afterlife, and the emergence of the next generation, life has continued into the present day, and so it shall always.

The veneration of Wesir in the modern day looks very different to his cults in the ancient world, within and outside of Egypt. Our cult practices usually reside within the confines of our homes and domestic shrines, rather than in grandiose temples. But much like our ancient counterparts, we light candles and burn incense at these shrines, which may be decorated with the likenesses of our ancestors and Divine icons that imitate ancient reliefs and sculptures. We extend prayers to Wesir, using epithets spoken by ancient tongues, reciting translated prayers, and creating our own. We light lamps, read the myths, raise miniature Djed Pillars, and contemplate Wesir's death and rebirth at seasonal festivals. Many of us plant seeds and watch them sprout in the sunlight and recede back into the earth when their time is complete. We attend funerals and mourn our departed loved ones, affirming that we will be reunited someday. So, Wesir's cult looks different today, but there are also many examples attesting to the revival of the Old Ways. We reach across time and geography to connect with where Wesir's cult left off, repairing the gap in the centuries that separate us. We have become the Two Kites, the funerary Goddesses of rebirth, who have returned Wesir to life in the modern day. Through our revived veneration, Wesir has once again been reborn. And so, may we continue to speak his name and to remember those who came before us.

Say their names and they shall live forever, and ever.

Appendix

Egyptian and Greek Deity Names

Included here are the names of ancient Egyptian Netjeru who are more commonly known today in their Greek form. For ease of a suggested pronunciation, I have written the Egyptian phonetically in the middle column, though it should be noted that accurate pronunciation is not certain due to the lack of vowels in the written language.

NAMES		
Transliteration	**Egyptian**	**Greek**
ꜣs.t	Aset	Isis (Goddess)
ḏḥwty	Djehuty	Thoth (God)
ḥwt-ḥr / ḥwt-ḥr.t	Hut-hor / Hut-herut	Hathor (Goddess)
ḥrw-wr	Heru-wer (also just Heru)	Horus the Elder (God)
ḥrw-sꜣ-ꜣs.t	Heru-sa-aset (also just Heru)	Horus son of Isis (God)
nb.t-hwt	Nebet-hut	Nephthys
stẖ	Sutekh / Set	Typhon (God)
wsjr	Wesir	Osiris (God)

Bibliography

Primary Sources

Ammianus Marcellinus *The Roman History, Book 22*, available at <https://penelope.uchicago.edu/Thayer/E/Roman/Texts/Ammian/22*.html> [accessed 10/12/24]

Book of the Dead, Chapter 6; trans. by University College London, available at <https://www.ucl.ac.uk/museums-static/digitalegypt/literature/religious/bd6.html> [accessed 10/12/24]

Borghouts, John. F., *Ancient Egyptian Magical Texts* (Leiden: Brill, 1978)

British Museum, *accession no. EA10471-21*, available at <https://www.britishmuseum.org/collection/object/Y_EA10471-21> [accessed 10/12/24]

Diodorus Siculus *Library of History*, available at <https://penelope.uchicago.edu/Thayer/E/Roman/Texts/Diodorus_Siculus/> [accessed 10/12/24]

Faulkner, Raymond O. (1969) *The Ancient Egyptian Pyramid Texts: Translated into English*, Oxford, The Clarendon Press

Faulkner, Raymond O. (1936) 'The Bremner-Rhind Papyrus: I. A. The Songs of Isis and Nephthys', *The Journal of Egyptian Archaeology*, vol. 22, no. 2, pp. 121–140

Faulkner, Raymond O. (1977) *The Ancient Egyptian Coffin Texts, Vol II Spells 355–787*, Warminster, Aris & Phillips Ltd

Orphic Fragment 237; trans. by James R. Van Kollenburg, available at <https://www.hellenicgods.org/orphic-fragment-237---otto-kern> [accessed 10/12/24]

Plutarch *Moralia, Vol. 5, 'Isis and Osiris'*; trans. F. C. Babbitt (1936) Cambridge, MA, Harvard University Press

The Lamentations of Isis and Nephthys (*P. Berlin 3008*); trans. by R. O. Faulkner, available at <https://www.attalus.org/egypt/lamentations.html> [accessed 10/12/24]

The Songs of Isis and Nephthys (BM EA 10188); trans. by R. O. Faulkner, available at <https://www.attalus.org/egypt/isis_nephthys.html> [accessed 10/12/24]

Dieter Betz, Hans, ed., (1986) The Greek Magical Papyri in Translation Including the Demotic Spells, Chicago, The University of Chicago Press

Secondary Sources

Abd Alrahman, M. H. M. (2020) 'The Astral and Solar Destinies of the Deceased in the Ancient Egyptian Texts' in *Journal of the Faculty of Tourism and Hotels-University of Sadat City*, 4.2/1: 24–40

Adams, Barbara and Krzysztof M. Ciałowicz (1997) *Protodynastic Egypt*, Buckinghamshire, Shire Egyptology

Allen, James P. (2015) *The ancient Egyptian pyramid texts [translated] by James P. Allen*, Atlanta, SBL Press

Ashby, Solange (2019) 'Milk Libations for Osiris. Nubian Piety at Philae', *Near Eastern Archaeology*, 82.4: 200–209

Betrò, Marilina (2024) 'Osirian Materia Sacra: A Glance from Corn-Mummies' *Religions*, 15.813: 1–21 <https://doi.org/10.3390/rel15070813>

Brewer, D. and Teeter, E. (2007) *Egypt and the Egyptians*, Cambridge, Cambridge University Press.

Brotto, Alice (2015) *The Death of Ancient Egyptian Gods: Terminological and Semantic Analysis of Literary evidence*, unpublished doctoral thesis, Università Degli Studi Di Pisa

Budde, Dagmar (2011) 'Epithets, Divine', in *UCLA Encyclopedia of Egyptology* (ed. by Jacco Dieleman and Willeke Wendrich), available at <http://digital2.library.ucla.edu/viewItem.do?ark=21198/zz0028t1z4> [accessed 10/12/24)

Centrone, M. C. (2004) *Egyptian Corn Mummies*, unpublished doctoral thesis, Swansea, University of Wales Swansea

Coulton, L., Hallmann, A., & Payraudeau, F. (2018) 'The Osirian Chapels at Karnak: An Historical and Art Historical Overview

Based on Recent Fieldwork and Studies, co-authored with Laurent Coulton and Frédéric Payraudeau', in *Thebes in the First Millennium BC: Art and Archaeology of the Kushite Period and Beyond* (ed. by E. Pischikova, J. Budka, & K. Griffin), London, Golden House Publications, pp. 271–293

Darby, W., Ghalioungui, P. & Grivetti, L. (1977) *Food: The Gift of Osiris, Vol. I*, London: Academic Press

David, Rosalie (2018) *Temple Ritual at Abydos*, London, The Egypt Exploration Society

Dekoulakou, India (2011a) 'Le sactuaire des dieux égyptiens à Marathon', in *Bibliotheca Isiaca II* (ed. by L. Bricault and R. Veymiers), Bordeaux, Ausonius, pp. 23–46

Dekoulakou, India (2011b) 'The Egyptian Sanctuary at Marathon', in *Second Hellenistic Studies Workshop, Alexandria, 4–11 July 2010: Proceedings* (ed. by Kyriakos Savvopoulos), Alexandria, Bibliotheca Alexandria, pp. 22–44

Delia, D. (1992) 'The Refreshing Water of Osiris', *Journal of the American Research Centre in Egypt*, 29: 181–190

El Din Anwar, Hossam (2019) 'The Religious Festivals in Ancient Egypt', in *Egyptian Journal of Tourism and Hospitality*, 26.2(1): 1–22

Farrar, J. & Farrar, S. (1984) *A Witches Bible: The Complete Witches' Handbook*, London: Robert Hale Ltd

First, Grzegorz, (2009) 'The Ptah-Sokar-Osiris Statues in the Cracow Collections', in *Studies in Ancient Art and Civilisation, vol. 13*, Kraków, Jagiellonian University, pp. 119–139

Frazer, James (1993) *The Golden Bough*, Ware, Wordsworth Ltd

Geisen, Christina (2012) *The Ramesseum Dramatic Papyrus. A New Edition, Translation, and Interpretation*, unpublished doctoral thesis, Toronto, University of Toronto

Griffiths, J. G. (1980) *The Origins of Osiris and His Cult*, Leiden, E. J. Brill

Guasch-Jané, M. R., Fonseca, S. & Ibrahim, M. (2013) '"Irep en Kemet" Wine of Ancient Egypt: Documenting the Viticulture and Winemaking Scenes in the Egyptian Tombs', in *ISPRS Annals of the Photogrammetry, Remote Sensing and Spatial Information Sciences*, 2.5: 157–161

Håland, Evy Johanne (2023) *Women, Pilgrimage, and Rituals of Healing in Modern and Ancient Greece: A Comparison*, Newcastle upon Tyne, Cambridge Scholars Publishing

Hornung, Erik (1996) *Conceptions of God in ancient Egypt: The one and the many* (trans. by J. Baines), Ithaca, Cornell University Press

Hornung, Erik (1999) *The Ancient Egyptian Books of the Afterlife* (trans. by David Lorton), Ithaca, Cornell University Press

Ikram, Salima (2003) *Death and Burial in Ancient Egypt*, London, Pearson Education

Ikram, Salima (2005) 'Divine Creatures: Animal Mummies', in *Divine Creatures, Animal Mummies in Ancient Egypt* (ed. by Salima Ikram), Cairo, The American University in Cairo Press, pp. 1–15

Jauhiainen, Heidi (2009) *"Do not celebrate your feast without your neighbours" A Study of References to Feasts and Festivals in Non-Literary Documents from Ramesside Period Deir el-Medina*, unpublished doctoral thesis, Helsinki, University of Helsinki

Kahl, Jochem (2007), *"Ra is My Lord:" Searching for the Rise of the Sun God at the Dawn of Egyptian History*, Harrassowitz Verlag, Wiesbaden

Kelly Simpson, William et al. (2003) 'Book of the Dead 125: "The Negative Confession"', in *The Literature of Ancient Egypt: An Anthology of Stories, Instructions, Stelae, Autobiographies, and Poetry* (Third Edition) (ed. by William Kelly Simpson), London, Yale University Press, pp. 267–277

Kinsman, O. (2015) 'A discussion on the function, structure and nature of the mwt within the category of ancient Egyptian demons', *Gorffennol*, 2: 83–100.

Lerner, L. (2019) 'Oriental Institute excavation at Tell Edfu reveals early New Kingdom complex', *UChicago News* <https://news.

uchicago.edu/story/ancient-urban-villa-shrine-ancestor-worship-discovered-egypt> [accessed 10/12/2024]

Lichtheim, Miriam (1973) *Ancient Egyptian Literature, Volume I: The Old and Middle Kingdoms,* Berkeley, University of California Press

Lichtheim, Miriam (1976) *Ancient Egyptian Literature, Volume II: The New Kingdom,* Berkeley, University of California Press

Malaise, Michel (1972) *Les Conditions de pénétration et de diffusion des cultes égyptiens en Italie,* Leiden, Brill

Malek, J. (2003) 'The Old Kingdom', in *The Oxford History of Ancient Egypt* (ed. by Ian Shaw), Oxford, Oxford University Press, pp. 83–107

Mazurek, Lindsey A. (2018) 'Middle Platonic Isis at Herodes Atticus' Marathon Villa', *American Journal of Archaeology,* 122.4: 611–644

Meeks, D. and Favard-Meeks, C., (1996) *Daily life of the Egyptian Gods* (trans. by G. M. Goshgarian), London, Pimlico

Mu-Chou, Poo (2009) *Wine and Wine Offering in the Religion of Ancient Egypt,* New York, Routledge

Naydler, Jeremy (2004) *Shamanic Wisdom in the Pyramid Texts: The Mystical Tradition of Ancient Egypt* (Rochester VT: Inner Traditions)

Oakes, L. (2006) *Sacred Sites of Ancient Egypt,* London, Hermes House

O'Connor, D. (2011) *Abydos: Egypt's First Pharaohs and the Cult of Osiris,* London, Thames & Hudson

Parkinson, R. (1991) *Voices from Ancient Egypt: An Anthology of Middle Kingdom Writings,* London, British Museum Press

Petacchi, S. (2024) 'The Evidence of Osiris Lord of Neheh-Eternity in Amun Temple B 700 at the Sacred Town of Gebel Barkal, Sudan', *Journal of Ancient Near Eastern Religions,* 24.1: 98–125, available at <https://doi.org/10.1163/15692124-12341344> [accessed 10/12/24]

Pinch, Geraldine (2002) *Egyptian Mythology. A guide to the Gods, Goddesses and Traditions of Ancient Egypt,* Oxford, Oxford University Press

Ragueh, Cherine Abou Zeid (2016) 'The blessing of grain represented in god 'Nepri' and his affiliate gods of grain: 'Osiris' and 'Renenutet', *Journal of the Association of Arab Universities for Tourism and Hospitality,* 13.2: 1–22

Raven, Maarten (2012) *Egyptian Magic. The Quest for Thoth's Book of Secrets,* Cairo, The American University in Cairo Press

Ritner, Robert (2008) *The Mechanics of Ancient Egyptian Magical Practice,* Chicago, The Oriental Institute of the University of Chicago

Roberts, Alison (2000) *My Heart My Mother: Death and Rebirth in Ancient Egypt,* Rottingdean, Northgate Publishers

Shaw, I. (2003) *The Oxford history of ancient Egypt edited by Ian Shaw,* Oxford, Oxford University Press

Shaw, I. and Nicholson, P. (2008) *The British Museum Dictionary Of Ancient Egypt,* London, British Museum Press

Smith, Mark (2017) *Following Osiris: Perspectives on the Osirian Afterlife from Four Millennia,* Oxford, Oxford University Press

Troche, J. (2018) 'Letters to the Dead', *UCLA Encyclopedia of Egyptology,* 1.1: 1–14

Uranić, Igor (2018) 'The Book of the Amduaton Papyrus Zagreb E-605', in *Vjesnik Arheološkog muzeja u Zagrebu,* 51.1: 55–66

van Dijk, J. (1986) 'The Symbolism of the Memphite Djed-Pillar', *OMRO,* 66: 7–20

van Dijk, J. (1989) 'An Early Hymn to Osiris as Nocturnal Manifestation of Re', in *The Memphite Tomb of Horemheb, Commander-in-Chief of Tutankhamun Part I: The Reliefs, Inscriptions, and Commentary* (ed. by Geoffrey T. Martin), London, Egypt Exploration Society, pp. 61–69.

Vickery, John B. (1973) *The Literary Impact of the Golden Bough,* Princeton, Princeton University Press

Wilkinson, Richard (2000) *The Complete Temples of Ancient Egypt*, London, Thames & Hudson

Wilkinson, Richard (2003) *The Complete Gods and Goddesses of Ancient Egypt*, London, Thames & Hudson

Zinn, Katharina (2013) 'Magic, Pharaonic Egypt', in *The Encyclopedia of Ancient History* (First Edition) (ed. by Roger S. Bagnall, Kai Brodersen, Craige B. Champion, Andrew Erskine, and Sabine R. Huebner), London, Blackwell Publishing Ltd, pp. 4227–4231

MOON BOOKS

PAGANISM & SHAMANISM

What is Paganism? A religion, a spirituality, an alternative belief system, nature worship? You can fi nd support for all these definitions (and many more) in dictionaries, encyclopaedias, and text books of religion, but subscribe to any one and the truth will evade you. Above all Paganism is a creative pursuit, an encounter with reality, an exploration of meaning and an expression of the soul. Druids, Heathens, Wiccans and others, all contribute their insights and literary riches to the Pagan tradition. Moon Books invites you to begin or to deepen your own encounter, right here, right now.

If you have enjoyed this book, why not tell other readers by posting a review on your preferred book site.

Bestsellers from Moon Books
Pagan Portals Series

The Morrigan

Meeting the Great Queens

Morgan Daimler

Ancient and enigmatic, the Morrigan reaches out to us. On shadowed wings and in raven's call, meet the ancient Irish goddess of war, battle, prophecy, death, sovereignty, and magic.

Paperback: 978-1-78279-833-0 ebook: 978-1-78279-834-7

The Awen Alone

Walking the Path of the Solitary Druid

Joanna van der Hoeven

An introductory guide for the solitary Druid, The Awen Alone will accompany you as you explore, and seek out your own place within the natural world.

Paperback: 978-1-78279-547-6 ebook: 978-1-78279-546-9

Moon Magic

Rachel Patterson

An introduction to working with the phases of the Moon, what they are and how to live in harmony with the lunar year and to utilise all the magical powers it provides.

Paperback: 978-1-78279-281-9 ebook: 978-1-78279-282-6

Hekate

A Devotional

Vivienne Moss

Hekate, Queen of Witches and the Shadow-Lands, haunts the pages of this devotional bringing magic and enchantment into your lives.

Paperback: 978-1-78535-161-7 ebook: 978-1-78535-162-4

Bestsellers from Moon Books

Keeping Her Keys

An Introduction to Hekate's Modern Witchcraft

Cyndi Brannen

Blending Hekate, witchcraft and personal development together to create

a powerful new magickal perspective.

Paperback: 978-1-78904-075-3 ebook 978-1-78904-076-0

Journey to the Dark Goddess

How to Return to Your Soul

Jane Meredith

Discover the powerful secrets of the Dark Goddess and transform your depression, grief and pain into healing and integration.

Paperback: 978-1-84694-677-6 ebook: 978-1-78099-223-5

Shamanic Reiki

Expanded Ways of Working with Universal Life Force Energy

Llyn Roberts, Robert Levy

Shamanism and Reiki are each powerful ways of healing; together, their power multiplies. Shamanic Reiki introduces techniques to help healers and Reiki practitioners tap ancient healing wisdom.

Paperback: 978-1-84694-037-8 ebook: 978-1-84694-650-9

Southern Cunning

Folkloric Witchcraft in the American South

Aaron Oberon

Modern witchcraft with a Southern flair, this book is a journey through the folklore of the American South and a look at the power these stories hold for modern witches.

Paperback: 978-1-78904-196-5 ebook: 978-1-78904-197-2

Readers of ebooks can buy or view any of these bestsellers by clicking on the live link in the title. Most titles are published in paperback and as an ebook. Paperbacks are available in traditional bookshops. Both print and ebook formats are available online.

Find more titles and sign up to our readers' newsletter www.collectiveinkbooks.com/paganism

For video content, author interviews and more, please subscribe to our YouTube channel.

MoonBooksPublishing

Follow us on social media for book news, promotions and more:

Facebook: Moon Books

Instagram: @MoonBooksCI

X: @MoonBooksCI

TikTok: @MoonBooksCI